#TheWalk
by Brian Branam

Scott and Loretta,

To the greatest staff family
I never knew... I'm not
bitter! :) God bless you all as you
now walk as grandparents!

Step by step.

Col 2:20

Cover Design: Brian Branam
Cover Image: James Eberlein
Chapter icon photos: Andre Haveman, Robyn Mackenzie, Mateusz Stachowski, Stephanie Berghaeuser, Martina, George Georgiades, Akiminki, Zsuzsanna Kilian, Nicole N
First Printing 2014
Printed in the United States of America
Scripture references marked ESV are taken from The Holy Bible, English Standard Version® (ESV®) Copyright © 2001 by Crossway, a publishing ministry of Good News Publishers. Used by permission. All rights reserved.

Distributed by Createspace, An Amazon Company

ISBN-13:978-1502472335

ISBN-10:1502472333

Dedication:

To my wife Shannon, who always brings me light when my mind wants to focus on the dark. You have loved me, inspired me, and lifted me up when I wanted to give up. I have experienced Christ in you.

To my daughters, Morgan and Kiley, who have softened my heart and inspired my walk. Because of you I finally understand God's love for me as Father. There is no volume of theology or commentary that has ever been written that has explained God's passion for His people like the two of you have revealed for me.

To my parents, Ernest and Brenda, who provided for me a consistent environment in which I could know Christ and paid an incalculable price for me to be who I am and do what I do.

To a praying grandmother who asked God to call a preacher from her generations.

Acknowledgments

It has always been my goal to write a book. I have started many, but often lose confidence and flounder toward an incomplete pile of unfinished thoughts. With *The Walk*, I have now completed one.

I count the accomplishment of this personal goal as a podium moment much like an induction speech for a baseball player into the Hall of Fame. Not so much as in the celebration of a quality accomplishment, as I do not see myself as a Hall of Famer, nor even this book in the pantheon of history's marquee achievements, but in the sense of I'm going to stand here and blubber for awhile and everyone else has to listen to me talk about people you don't know. You may not know these people, but they have been formative for me.

You may not choose to read on from this point, but there is a takeaway on this page for all of us. **Never underestimate the power of your influence.** There is a call on each of our lives to inspire others to go further (Hebrews 10:24).

I want to thank some great friends who have been loyal to me from very early on: Dell Cornett, Chris Altman, Dave Delmotte.

I want to thank Ms. Thelma for making me promise to keep working hard to improve. I graduated from seminary. I finished a book. I will not stop. I miss you so much.

I want to thank my pastor, Dr. Wayne Hamrick who gave me an opportunity, taught me how to be a pastor, and always paid attention to the details. You drove me crazy, but you prevented me from ever being satisfied with good. You always pushed me toward great. The chairs in the fellowship hall are straight.

I want to thank Mrs. Joan Hamrick for providing me an example of the kind of lady I needed to search for as a wife if I was going to give my life to serving the church.

I want to thank a handful of men who poured into me at critical times along the way: Ron Bishop, Doug Sager, Bradley Price, and Frank Cox.

I want to thank Pat Bishop for teaching me that God has a plan for my life. That truth changed everything for me.

I want to thank Glenn Deakins for telling me I was going on a mission trip to Russia and not asking if I wanted to go. Sometimes you've just got to go to know.

I want to thank two godly women who I know are praying for me, Mary Dobbins and Cecilia Cooper.

I want to thank Rod and Robin McSweeney for providing a blessed place to escape from the world and work on a book. Rod, thank you for your friendship and for just allowing me to sit in your office and listen to you talk about anything. I learned a ton from you in what I know was a difficult season of your life.

I want to thank Johnny Kilgore for being an example of humility, faithfulness, and loyalty to a pastor and a church.

Thank you Linda Marcrum for taking the time to proof this manuscript and redeem the words.

To every member of the churches I served as pastor who never quit, continued to work, and believed strongly in a God who can turn any situation into victory.

I want to thank my home church, New Liberty Baptist in Ringgold, Georgia for loving and valuing me as a child.

I want to especially thank the church I currently serve as pastor, Liberty Baptist Church in Dalton, Georgia for being supportive and prayerful through this process.

To every person who said, "I want a copy." You kept me going.

Table of Contents

Why Walk?

Keep steady my steps according to your promise, and let no iniquity get dominion over me (Psalm 119:133 ESV).

Do you want to go faster or further? In the Olympic games there are plenty of events in which success is achieved by the ones who go faster. Our culture conditions us to do life faster. The problem is that a successful life requires one to go further.

Your family does not need you to go any faster. Your family needs you to go further.

If you are someone who has faith in Christ, let me warn you: *it's not about how you start, but about how you finish*. You may look great coming out of the gate, but following Christ demands that you also be there in the end.

If you are married, fast doesn't do well for a race that is to be run until death do us part. A few years of great romance does not carry enough equity for the spouse that feels emotionally abandoned after nearly a decade of marriage. You may have started great, but if you do not keep stride in your marriage, it will not end well.

In business very few are instantly successful, and for those that are, the landscape is littered with the "has-been." Lots of people come out of the gate fast, but the successful ones are still running.

Have you ever heard anyone celebrate a fast friendship? We value the friends who are loyal. We want a friend who will go further.

We all know someone in some venue of life who started well, showed some promise, but didn't get very far. We probably also have another acquaintance in common. You know the person. The one who seemed to make a major turn, even professed faith in Christ. Their start was remarkable, but it didn't last very long. Their flash of faith went fast, not far.

Bobby Bowden was a Division 1A college football coach for 40 years. Off the top of your head, what can you write on a piece of paper about his first 10 wins? Probably nothing. Even if his first 10 wins were blowouts and he looked like a brilliant young up and coming coach in each of them, does it really matter, good or bad, what people were saying about the man in his first 10 wins?

If I asked even a novice sports fan to take that same piece of paper and write what they knew about Bobby Bowden, the words "winningest coach of all time" would certainly make the page. Bobby Bowden is not celebrated for how fast he went, but how far. Nobody talks about how the winningest coach of all time started. Anybody who talks about the man refers to WHERE he finished: 377 wins.

Think of how many college football coaches during Bobby Bowden's career were a flash in the pan. Think of how many great hires were made during Bowden's career that became headline "fires" after a sub-par season. Most coaches look stellar at their first press conference as they express gratitude for the opportunity to be at such a great school and their desire to continue the winning tradition. The problem is that press conferences may help a new coach score points with the media, but they put no points on the board in games.

Your family, your faith, your friends, your work . . . they don't need a polished press conference from you. Your family, your faith, your friends, your work . . . they hear your promises, but they need you to actually score points. Your family, your faith, your friends, your work . . . nobody will be satisfied if you have only one or two great seasons. The people closest to you and the things in your life you influence the most need more from you. These people and these things need you to go far.

The problem is that we are going too fast to go far.

I may lose you immediately, but there are a lot of books that are about helping you do more. Not this one. There are a lot of books about helping you do what you do faster. Not this one. This book is counterintuitive to every demand you experience in your busy life. This book is actually about slowing down and doing less. This book is about lengthening not shortening. This book is about going further.

The breakneck speed at which we do life has made one of the Bible's most profound concepts almost foreign to us: *Walk*.

We are driving, texting, talking, networking, and updating. Our pathways are guided by intricate systems which communicate our exact coordinates to global positioning satellites instantaneously. We are told where to turn and exactly what time we are projected to arrive at our destination. We do life at smartphone speed.

When the writers of Scripture describe life, you can tell that they lived at a different pace. They frequently use words like "walk" and "step." When Paul says repeatedly in his letters for us to *"walk worthy"* (Ephesians 4:1 or Col. 1:10), he is not only admonishing his readers to pay attention to how they live, but he is naturally reflecting their speed of life. They walked everywhere they went. Walking was so common it was an action that became synonymous with life.

David says in Psalm 37:23 that the "steps of a man are established by the Lord." In Psalm 119 the Word of God is illumination for the writer's feet and a light for his path. The proximity of the verse describing a light at one's feet suggests life at close range, at walking pace.

Because we have grown accustomed to life at digital speeds, we want instantaneous results. Yet we forget. We may be able to Google information from almost anywhere, but we cannot Google a life-long relationship with God.

Guided by GPS, we can arrive at any destination and have no idea how we got there. Long life with the Lord is not merely about arrival at a destination, it is about steps. It is less about praying about where we want to be and more about paying attention to where we are and how what the Bible says applies to today.

Living at smartphone speed, we are deceived to believe we need all the answers. If you want to go further, do what David did in Psalm 37:23. Do life at a walking pace, with the Word of God in hand to light the path before your feet. If you live like that, you don't need all the answers, you need only one. What's the next step?

We need to be asking more questions like "What's next?" rather than questions that begin with "When?" Your phone may know exactly "when" you will arrive, but God is less concerned with the "when" and more concerned with the "way" you get there. At one time the Christian life was actually known as "*the Way*" (Acts 9:2). Living long for God has never been referred to as "*the When*."

In the past, we asked for directions. Now all we want is an address. Not so long ago we received directions based on scenic landmarks: "Turn at the barn just over the hill. There is a massive oak tree in a field. You'll see Calfee's store. You can't miss it." Now we drive to a coordinate on a map and miss everything along the way.

The Bible wants you to see what's along the way and take time to think about why it is there, who built it, who lives there, what's the story, and what everything you see says about the next step.

We may live a multi-tasking *digi'* life, but somehow we need to break it down. We especially need to break down our journey with the Lord, into steps.

Slow it down. Be deliberate with the day. Become less frustrated with where you want to be, and more intentional about where you are.

———————

For me, my 40th birthday brought with it less celebration of what I have done and more anguish over what I haven't. I am very driven but at times not very direct. I am a visionary who has no patience for details.

Vision without details is like the dreams you have at night. They are very real, but they never actually become a reality outside of your head.

At 40 there is this sobering realization that there may be less life in front of you than there is behind. Some people refer to this as the "mid-life crisis." Most people at this juncture of time start buying really nice, self-indulgent things. If this truly is my mid-point, I can't afford it!

So I have a lot of unfulfilled expectations and goals still out there ahead of me, but a lingering feeling that there may not be enough time. There are many good things about my life I enjoy, but there are also some real points of frustration over where I am with some goals I had set for myself long ago. For me, 40 meant that it was time to get selective.

_____

One morning I was in study and began praying through a paragraph in Psalm 119. "Praying" may be too righteous a word. I was whining at God. I just happened to be whining through Psalm 119 that day.

I began at verse 129. "God, I believe your testimonies are wonderful and I have made it the focus of my soul to keep them. I preach because I believe the unfolding of your Words gives light and imparts understanding to the simple. Yet, I am not where I want to be in my preaching, writing, or teaching. The very things I feel like You have created, redeemed, and called me to do . . . I feel like I am lagging sorely behind." I said some other things at this juncture that were just frustratingly petty and whiny. Those things are not worthy to print. Then I prayed through verses 131 and 132, asking God, as the Psalmist did, to "turn to me and be gracious to me. I love your name, give me opportunity and favor. Please give me an opportunity to . . ."

In short, I Googled God. I asked for destination without any regard for the directions. Once again, vision was grossly lacking detail. I wanted to arrive. I cared nothing about asking God about how to get there.

At verse 133, God showed me something that has revolutionized my thinking ever since: _Steps_.

"Keep steady my steps according to your promise, and let no iniquity get dominion over me - Psalm 119:133 (ESV)."

I suddenly realized that God is less concerned with supplying an answer than He is about pointing the way. He is not a God of destinations as much as He is the Sovereign of our steps.

As I meditated on that verse a revolutionary truth began to flood my soul. What if I kept my goals before me, but instead of asking God to grant me my desired destinations, instead I asked Him to show me my steps. What if I became less concerned about what hasn't happened and why, and more concerned with what is happening - and what it means. My focus changed from being less concerned with where I want to be tomorrow and more intentional about the one step I can take today.

My problem has always been that I want to achieve everything fast. I wanted to break the tape without the run. For 40 years I have been standing, staring at the finish line, wanting more than anything to be there ignoring the simple reason I am still here. No steps. Truth is, it took me 40 years to realize I haven't made it very far.

My wife Shannon often says that God speaks in themes. It's crazy how at times God has been speaking to us about something and we will read about it in the Bible, we will hear it on the radio, it will come up randomly in conversation, and inevitably something will happen in our church related to the idea. The teaching becomes inescapable. Whatever it is, it becomes a theme that resonates with everything we tend to be involved with at the time.

I finished the morning by doing a quick survey of the words "walk" and "steps" in the Bible. I created a list of verses and began reading through them. I went on about my day, thinking about the idea of "steps" and the commonality of the metaphor of "walking" in the Bible. I began to reshape my prayer life, focusing everything I asked God for, ultimately into one idea, "What is my next step? What do You want me to do today?"

Later that afternoon I sat down to do some future sermon planning. I called my friend Chris. We have been lifelong friends and he now serves as a student pastor in a town about three hours away from where we live. I have had the opportunity to preach at his student summer camps for the last seven years. "So what is the theme for this year?" I asked. Guess what Chris said.

"*Walk.*"

Since that day I have intensified my study of the theme of the *walk* in the Bible. In doing so, I discovered five prominent ideas the Bible teaches about *The Walk*.

1) The Bible often describes living a life that pleases God as "walking in His ways" (Micah 6:8). People who walk with God do more than satisfy a religious ritual. People who walk with God reflect God's heart in everything they do because they have at their heart the desire to please Him. People who go further don't spend inordinate amounts of time doing the things most people do. People who go further see the things most of us spend our time on as distractions. People who go far know what matters. Pass everything you do through the filter of pleasing God and see how much of what you think is essential and important to your life becomes a distraction. If you put pleasing God as the first priority of your life, what you think you can't live without will soon become the very things you can't wait to toss aside. Seek to please God and see how far you go with things that really matter.

    2) Our walk was ruined by sin (Gen. 3:8). The way Genesis 3:8 is written implies that it was the habit of God to meet with Adam and the woman in the garden and walk with them.

"And they heard the sound of the LORD God walking in the garden in the cool of the day, and the man and his wife hid themselves from the presence of the LORD God among the trees of the garden - Genesis 3:8 (ESV)"

    If you read the verse correctly, the unusual thing was not that God was walking, it was that Adam and his wife were hiding. We will explore this idea later in the book, but think of how much of our activity is motivated by hiding from God instead of walking with Him. We still hide in the bushes when God passes by. The only difference in us and the first couple, is we hide in the bushes with a phone constantly in our face.

    Adam and Eve were the first humans in history to be deceived into thinking faster is better (Gen. 3:5). They wanted vision but conveniently forgot the details (Gen. 2:16-17). They made a fast mistake and, as a result, their walk in the garden didn't go very far.

3) There is a great reward for everyone who walks with God (Gen. 5:24, Deut. 5:33). The Bible says in Genesis 5 that men began to call upon the name of the Lord, but one man went further. His name was Enoch. The Bible simply says that *"Enoch walked with God, and God took Him, for he was not."*

An important context of Genesis 5 is that the chapter reads like a death march. The most surprising death of all is that of Adam. It is an early, sinister reminder that because we have sinned, there is no escape from death. Yet, one man walked with God and was rewarded. He didn't die, God rescued him from death and simply took him. His bypassing death was the first indication that God's greatest gift to sinners was eternal life. For those who walk with God, it really is possible to live forever. Forever is as far as any of us want to go. But walking with Christ is not just about entering eternity later, it is about beginning to walk forever now.

Can you imagine the impact it would have on everything you do with your life if you weren't just planning for retirement, or trying to make it to the end of a project, or rushing toward the next appointment? What if you realized what you do and the way you do it could make a forever difference? Think about the difference it would make in the success of every decision if you began to consider not just its immediate consequence (fast), but you were able, with wisdom, to discern its lasting impact (far).

4) People who walk with God are able to make critical decisions at key moments and accomplish incredible things (Gen. 6:9, 1 Kings 3:6). Noah walked with God and it saved His family. Everyone else's life ended in the flood. Noah knew what to do and went further.

In 1 Kings 3:6 Solomon is invited by God to ask for anything he felt he needed that would help him govern his kingdom. Instead of grabbing hold of going fast, Solomon grabbed hold of going far. As he prays to God, Solomon recalls the example of his father David and says,

"You have shown great and steadfast love to your servant David my father, because he walked before you in faithfulness, in righteousness, and in uprightness of heart toward you. And you have kept for him this great and steadfast love and have given him a son to sit on his throne this day - 1 Kings 3:6 (ESV)."

I want my daughters to be able to say this about me - that they watched their father walk before God in faithfulness. I don't want them to talk about how fast I went, but how far. I don't want them to summarize my life by saying that I was busy. I want them to celebrate the things that I did that were lasting. I want them to remember the things I said, to see the fruit of the work I did, and to cherish the time I spent with them. Those are the things that will go a long way with our kids and with other people.

For Solomon, the example of a godly father helped him to make the most critical choice of his life. He did not ask God for wealth, but for wisdom. He did not ask for speed, but distance.

Because of his request, God honored him to become a king without equal. If you want to make great choices at critical moments that will help you go further, walk with God.

5) The decision to walk with God is life-altering. In the Bible, the word *walk* describes the way one does life. The word *walk* does not simply mean to put one foot in front of the other, *walk* describes the way we do everything we do. Walking is not about where we are going. Walking is about how we are getting there. Your walk is the way you go about life. The Bible seldom speaks of running. When it does, even then, it's a distance race (Heb. 12:1). The Bible is more concerned with walking. It is about going far, one step at a time.

In the rest of this book I want to share with you this Biblical concept of walking with God that has revolutionized my life. *If you will break life down into steps, you may not go faster, but you will go further.* We will look at eight concepts, each of them gleaned from what the Scriptures teach about walking with God. We will look at the importance of *Pace, Paths, Presence, Providence, Provision, Priority, Progress,* and *Plan* in making a long, successful journey.

No matter how much or how little life we have before us, I hope you will find what I have found. When I break life down into steps and walk with God, the things I do go further. By "further," I mean that the quality of the things I do improves significantly. The things I do have greater meaning, and these same things seem to positively influence more people. There is no more vision without execution. Walking demands that I pay greater attention to what's next instead of being constantly frustrated that I am not where I want to be.

Allow me to extend an invitation. Let's walk.

Pace

For everything there is a season, and a time for every matter under heaven - Ecclesiastes 3:1 (ESV).

As I studied the idea of the walk in Scripture, I found that God never does many of the things that are so characteristic of the pace at which I live. God never hurries. You will never find a verse in the Bible where God is running, trying to catch up to anything. He is never behind. With Him, there is no rush. If this is the pace of God, exactly where is it we think we are going moving so fast?

The term *Godspeed* is an old term people once used to wish someone well on a journey. What we want with the word is for God to go with us so that things will go well. What we seldom think about is that for God to go with us, we need to slow down. *God walks wherever He goes.*

If we walk with God, He will set the pace in three vital areas of life. He sets the pace of our day. He sets the pace of our presence. He sets the pace of our limitations.

The pace of my day

God is the prime mover, but He is not a fast mover. As prime mover, God set all things in motion. As a general mover, God is frustratingly slow. Two stories serve to demonstrate.

The pace of Luke 8 seems fast and furious. Jesus is healing. He is teaching. His family is looking for Him. He is caught in a turbulent storm that He calms while crossing the sea. He casts demons out of a maniac man who lives in a graveyard. There is a lot happening. The more He does, the more attention He draws and the crowd grows.

When it seems like the stories have reached fever pitch, Jairus, a ruler of the synagogue falls at Jesus' feet and asks Jesus to accompany him to his house. His twelve-year-old daughter is sick and dying. Jairus is desperate for Jesus to heal her. Jairus thinks he needs Jesus to move fast. Jesus is more interested in helping Jairus go far.

As much as Jesus has going on, He complies and begins the walk toward Jairus' home. The next part of the verse sets the scene, "As Jesus went, the people pressed around him" (Luke 8:42). Imagine a throng of people, each of whom has needs, vying for Jesus' attention as He walks. The scene is loud and chaotic.

All of the sudden, Jesus stops. Unknown to the crowd, a woman with a blood issue has touched the hem of Jesus' garment and is healed. She has dealt with this problem for twelve years and had spent all of her money on physicians who all failed to help her. Like Jairus, she is also desperate.

Her problem probably caused her to have a constant menstrual flow. An issue of blood in Jewish culture was not merely a physical problem, but a spiritually crippling one. Because of the flow of blood, she was constantly unclean and would not have been allowed to enter into the Temple for worship.

Jesus stops. Though the crowd has no idea of what happened, Jesus knows. With all that is going on, Jesus is able somehow to focus on one thing. (The Master is not a multi-tasker.)

In the midst of a throng of people that is described by Luke as a "press", Jesus addresses the crowd and asks a question: "Who was it that touched me?"

The Bible says that everyone in the crowd denied it, yet Jesus must have persisted to know. Peter, wanting to bring some logic to the situation, tells Jesus that it is impossible to know who touched Him. It is a press of people. A press is a group so large you have to keep moving, but you are stopping. Who touched You? Everyone is touching You!

Yet someone touched Jesus in a way that power came out of Him and He knew it. Eventually, the woman reveals herself, and Jesus simply says to her, "*Daughter, your faith has made you well; go in peace.*" - *Luke 8:48 (ESV)*

Luke records nothing of Jairus' reaction in this moment. As the father of two daughters, I cannot ignore the man. Luke says little of him in the scene at this point, but I can see him. Time is running out. In his mind the solution is in hand, but far from where it really needs to be. We must keep moving.

For a man who needs Jesus to move fast, walking would be difficult enough; stopping and taking the time to poll the crowd for a mystery toucher would have been excruciating. In Jairus' mind his total focus must have been on the fact that it appeared by stopping for the woman, Jesus was going nowhere.

It is inexplicable, but there are times in walking with God, that when it seems we need Him to move the most, He stops.

The progression to the next part of the scene is heartbreaking. The Bible says while Jesus was still speaking, as if He is putting the final touches on His statements about the triumph of the woman's faith, Jairus receives the most devastating news. A nameless woman in the crowd may have been healed, but "Jairus, your daughter is dead." The bearer of the bad news follows up his statement: "do not trouble the Teacher anymore."

Too late.

Too slow.

For the nameless woman, the stop was the beginning of new life. For Jairus, the stop appeared to be the end of life. Don't trouble the Teacher anymore. He's too busy dealing with other things.

The second story involves a close friend of Jesus named Lazarus and his sisters, Mary and Martha. Again, a message is sent to Jesus that someone is sick and dying. Again, Jesus delays. This time He doesn't delay to poll the audience for a few minutes. This time Jesus delays for two days. Most surprising of all, He waits until He knows Lazarus is dead (John 11:14).

If you read the conversation between Jesus and His apostles in John 11, it is the ultimate example of "lost in translation." Jesus is telling them plainly that what He has done is allow Lazarus to die so that He can raise Him to the glory of God and for the furtherance of their faith. They plainly have no idea what He is talking about. Why? Their problem is not with the language. Their problem is with the timing. We expect God to do what we would do when alerted of an emergency. Run. Rush. Get hectic. They didn't understand because the pace of godspeed was as foreign to them as it is to us.

You and I have less problem with what Jesus says than we do with how slowly and inconveniently He does what He does. Compounding the problem is not only the fact that Lazarus is dead, but that there are people in Bethany who want to kill Jesus and His posse. Had Lazarus merely been sick, the apostles would have understood if Jesus had hurried to heal him, but now that Lazarus is dead, why hurry? In fact, not only is Lazarus now gone, but a move toward Bethany also threatens death for them. Jesus has opposition waiting for Him there. So what does Jesus say, now that danger is on the horizon? Let's move.

Our faith is not lost in the language of the Bible. We understand the stories. Our faith is lost in the timing of our experiences. It is hard to have faith at such an awkward pace.

The apostles make it clear to Jesus. For Lazarus, it is too late. For us to move now, due to our enemies, it is not only too late, but much too dangerous. As if the conversation were not strange enough, Jesus replies to the apostles' objections with what appears to be a riddle:

"Are there not twelve hours in the day? If anyone walks in the day, he does not stumble, because he sees the light of this world. But if anyone walks in the night, he stumbles, because the light is not in him." - John 11:9-10 (ESV)

In other words, now that Lazarus is dead and now that there are plenty of people around him that want Jesus and His apostles dead, the timing is perfect. Just when the pace of it all breaks us, it is then that God begins to move.

The editorial note that John adds to his gospel is priceless. *"Now when Jesus came, he found that Lazarus had already been in the tomb four days. Bethany was near Jerusalem, about two miles off."* - John 11:17-18 (ESV)

Being only two miles away, Jesus could have jogged there in less than 20 minutes if the Son of God were in any kind of decent shape. But instead of a twenty-minute jog, Jesus has stretched two miles into 4 days. At this pace, Lazarus is not just dead, he is decaying.

As slow as God goes when He walks, what really blows our minds is when He stops. In both stories, if the lack of rush were not enough, it is the stopping that seems most illogical. Yet despite the slowing and the stopping, both stories end remarkably the same. Jesus eventually arrives, unhurried, and raises both Jairus' daughter and His friend Lazarus from the dead.

What brings both stories together in pace is not that Jesus raises both of them from the dead but what He teaches along the way. Both stories result in a miracle, but both stories are purposed upon not merely raising the dead, but upon furthering faith. It is as if Jesus is signaling to us that if He answers too fast, an opportunity is lost to add distance to our faith. In these circumstances it is as if He knew that if He heals the sick too fast, our faith won't get as far.

Jesus is frustratingly slow, but along the way he teaches lessons we didn't request and He does things you and I didn't ask Him to do. Those lessons are more important than the miracles themselves. Each day of the delay was a calculated choice of pace. You and I may be in a hurry to get God to do what He does, but He is simply walking. He is more intent on our listening to what he says along the way. If it takes a 2-mile-over-4-days pace for those lessons to be learned; so be it. *This is godspeed.*

Don't fret if it seems like time is running out. When you walk with a God who can raise the dead, you're never going to be late.

————

Have you ever thought about what God teaches us in the pace of creation? If God said, "Let there be light," and there was light, don't you think He could have just as easily have said, "Let there be a universe, fully furnished" and there would have been life as we know it? Yet it took Him six days to talk it out and work it out. If it took God six days to create the world, what is it that you and I think we can accomplish by trying to outpace Him in a week?

We must learn to do what God does - pace the day.

God has infused a rhythmic schedule into creation. It would benefit us greatly to walk accordingly. There is day and night. Some of us never quit, so God turns the lights out as a signal. The sun has gone down. So should you.

Get off of *Facebook*. Turn off the television. Stop working. Shut down the computer. Relax. Don't work. Talk. Tell the story of your day - God tells us the story of His. Go to bed.

If God waited until day 2 to create the heavens (Gen. 1:6-8), what is it that you and I have going on that can't possibly wait until tomorrow?

God invented the day off! After six days of creation, God rested. He not only rested on the Sabbath, but He sanctified the day and separated it for His people to come to Himself. Numerous studies have shown that people are more productive when they not only have something to look forward to, but when they have a scheduled day without work. A day off actually makes our days on more effective.

The industrial revolution brought with it the demand for factories to be running 24/7 in order to be productive. A 10-16 hour workday was the norm. Henry Ford revolutionized our thoughts about productivity by not only nearly doubling the pay of his workers, but asking them to work less: five 8-hour days or 40 hours per week, to be exact. Within two years Ford had doubled not only the productivity of his factories but also his profit margin. Ford said that in order to be productive, one had

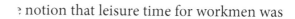

? notion that leisure time for workmen was

ᵤ... ᵣᵉ a rhythm to the world by giving us seasons. In certain seasons, certain things don't happen. To take it a step further, in certain seasons, certain things can't happen. The quicker you learn that you can't harvest in the winter, the less frustrated you will be about the pace of your life. Corn grows tall in July. It does nothing in January. The applications of this principle are endless.

Living in a commercial based economy instead of an agricultural one, we have lost the art of sowing and reaping. The grocery store is deceiving. In most markets you can buy strawberries year round. There is certainly no end to bananas! The problem is our grocery stores are a product of importing and exporting. There is no real observance of seasons at the supermarket. Yet we must realize in our pace that there is no season of harvest if there is not also a season of sowing. Importing and exporting may be fast, but for those who want a real harvest, the plan has to zero in on far. For the harvester it is necessary to know your season. There are seasons of watering, waiting, and dormancy. None of them are fast. Knowing them will help you go far. Learn to discern your season.

The pace of my presence

What do I mean by the pace of my presence? I mean the pace it takes for you to actually be present in the moment. The pace of your presence is the time it will cost to give your undivided attention.

Because we are living so fast, we are living extremely distracted. Studies have shown that in an image-driven, media-saturated society our ability to concentrate is diminishing. We need a pace that fosters presence.

The prophet Jeremiah is unusual. He is unusual not because of some sort of wild, outlandish visions or miracles. He is unusual because of his total lack of them. Ezekiel saw flaming wheels. Isaiah saw God on His throne. Daniel received visions that are more like comic books than sermons. Yet Jeremiah, saw nothing until the day God told him to take notice.

In Jeremiah 1 God asks the prophet a most profound question: "What do you see (Jer. 1:11)?" Jeremiah then begins to describe to God things that he sees every day. "I see an almond tree." "I see a man pouring out a boiling pot of water." Perhaps Jeremiah's most well known prophecy is that of the potter's wheel (Jeremiah 18). It is life changing vision inspired by a day at the potter's shop, watching a master at his craft. The message of Jeremiah that shook a nation came about by him simply taking notice of what was there as he walked.

He saw those things everyday, but when God told Jeremiah to notice them, the prophet never saw them the same way again.

What do you see?

I have a smartphone, so I can say this with authority. Technology is sucking the life out of our souls. *We need to take less notifications and we need to take more notice.* Our smartphones dumb us down with constant interruptions. Instead of time with God first thing in the morning we have to check email and receive status updates. Most of us can no longer sit still at a red light. Once the car is stopped, even for a minute or two, we immediately start flipping through apps and perusing our notifications. We receive more information at an intersection than our grandparents did in their lifetimes.

We get a lot of information but have lost the art of meditation. We know what is happening, but think very little of what it means. Those who want to go further must also go deeper. We have to notice the almond trees. When was the last time you read something from the Bible and thought about it the entire day? When was the last time something you read in the Bible changed the way you saw things throughout the day? If the brain is constantly interrupted by notifications, giving proper attention to deeper truth is impossible.

Because we are at a place in time and technology in which we want to know so much, we have reached a place in which I believe we know too much. The fast pace at which we receive notifications is causing the erosion of one of our greatest God given abilities - the ability to think. We no longer take time to think about what we know.

Isaiah 26:3 says, "*You keep him in perfect peace whose mind is stayed on you, because he trusts in you.*" With constant notifications we are not at a pace for peace. It is difficult to get our minds to "stay" on the Lord when it strays after every vibration and alert that comes through our smartphone.

Kevin Deyoung offers sage advice in his helpful book, *Crazy Busy, A (Mercifully) Short Book about a (Really) Big Problem*. He says that the "screen is strangling *our* soul."[1] He says that not only is there an issue with addiction when it comes to our technology, but an issue he calls *acedia*. According to Deyoung, *acedia* is an old word that means "sloth" or "laziness." Deyoung goes on to say,

> *For too many of us, the hustle and bustle of electronic activity is a sad expression of a deeper acedia. We feel busy, but not with a hobby or recreation or play. We are busy with busyness. Rather than figure out what to do with our spare minutes and hours, we are content to swim in the shallows and pass our time with passing the time. How many of us, growing too accustomed to the acedia of our age, feel this strange mix of busyness and lifelessness? We are always engaged with our thumbs, but rarely engaged with our thoughts. We keep downloading information, but rarely get down into the depths of our hearts. That's acedia— purposelessness disguised as constant commotion.*[2]

By being in the shallows of constant commotion, we miss the profound lesson of the almond tree. Unlike Jeremiah, we stop at a red light and see nothing because we are in a frivolous attempt to know everything.

I'll be the first to admit that I have a damaged attention span. I'm addicted to notification. As soon as I feel the vibration or hear the tone, no matter who I am with or what I am doing, I have an insatiable need to know what it is about. Recently, I have designated strategic times to be without my phone. This sounds crazy to think of this as a sacrificial act, because I can remember a time when I spent most of my day with no access to a phone (I know I am dating myself here). Somehow, I survived.

Early in the morning I try to reserve time for Scripture reading and prayer. I do not use any sort of device to accomplish this task. As much as we enjoy having several versions of the Bible easily accessed on our device, most of which include some sort of Scripture reading plan, let's be honest. We still get notifications from other apps. It is way too tempting to peal away from the Word and check them. So, in the morning, I go old school - paper version of the Bible and a pen.

When I am at a restaurant with my family, I try to leave my phone in the car as often as I can. I challenge you to do a quick visual survey of the other patrons in the next restaurant you visit. Notice how many couples, families, and/or friends are not talking but rather sitting across the table from one another with a phone in their face. They are receiving notifications from people that may be miles away, but totally ignoring the person or the people in their presence.

If you have children, your influence will go further with them than it will with anyone else. There is not another person on the planet that God has ordained to model what they see in you like He has your children. They are your greatest opportunity to add distance to the legacy of your life. What you say to your kids will go a long way with them. If you constantly have a phone in your face, they'll remember that too.

I think at a deeper level we are doing with our devices what Adam and the woman did when God came to them walking in the garden. We are hiding from Him rather than walking with Him. Being notification busy is a convenient way of escaping the more critical tasks of Bible reading, reflection, prayer, confession, and discernment. If I concentrate on knowing everyone else's status, I don't have to deal with what God is trying to show me about my own. If I get caught up in everyone else's walk, I can't possibly concentrate on the step God is calling me to take today.

It seems like you can deal with what everyone else is doing much faster than you can deal with what is actually in front of you. With your social network friends, you can like it and move on. But remember, your real friends don't need you to go faster, they need you to go further. You need to pace your presence.

The pace of my limitations

I am an only child, a spoiled brat, a control freak. I am egocentric. It is extremely difficult for me to see my limitations. I know they are there because, as I said in the opening pages of the book, I am more frustrated by what I haven't done than I am satisfied by what I have.

Being a pastor only exacerbates this problem. My day is a flurry of interruptions, distractions, and requests. On top of the frustration that I can't possibly deal with every request is the egomaniacal comparisons that pastors make to one another. There is always someone out there doing it better than you. They are the ones speaking at the conferences. You are usually always the guy paying $100 to sit in the seat and listen to how perfect his life is. I don't leave those meetings encouraged. I usually leave them exhausted.

When you are trapped in the game of comparisons, your pace quickens as you try to catch up to the tasks you need to accomplish, while also frivolously trying to catch up to everyone else's accomplishments. Being the best means you have to be fast. You try harder to move quicker. Soon you are flying, but you are also dying. You can't catch them and you feel incompetent and worthless. Fast won't get you far.

While studying this idea of the walk, the Spirit led me to an incredibly freeing thought. God is not nearly as aggravated by my limitations as I am.

God doesn't expect us to catch up with anyone. He expects us only to stay with Him. He is looking only for us to walk at godspeed. God walks everywhere He goes. It is remarkably easy to outrun the Almighty. The problem is that everyone who beats God in a foot race loses.

The Bible says that when Moses was 120 his eye was not dim and his vigor was unabated (Deuteronomy 34:7). I'm 40 and exhausted with it all. I can't imagine 80 more years living like I have lived the last 10. I'm tired now. How can a man possibly make it to 120 and be ready for more? How did he make it that far? He walked with God and stuttered the whole way.

In the infamous account of God's calling Moses that is recorded in Exodus 3 and 4, Moses objects to being God's prophet by saying, *"Oh, my Lord, I am not eloquent, either in the past or since you have spoken to your servant, but I am slow of speech and of tongue." - Exodus 4:10 (ESV).*

Don't miss the irony here. Moses was confessing to His Creator that he stutters. Why is it we feel the need to remind an all-knowing God of our limitations?

I love God's reply. In speaking back to Moses, the Lord did not stutter, but was perfectly clear with His question: "Who has made man's mouth?" God is well aware of our limitations.

God sends a message to His people through another prophet, Isaiah. Their hearts are hardened and they will soon reach the end of their limitations. Despite God's counsel, they will be defeated. Yet, God sends them an invitation to grace. Though they will fall, lifting them again is not beyond God's ability, *"But they who wait for the LORD shall renew their strength; they shall mount up with wings like eagles; they shall run and not be weary; they shall walk and not faint." - Isaiah 40:31 (ESV)*

I can't answer every email. I can't reply to every text message.
I can't possibly keep up with every update on social media. But I
can wait. I can say, "no." God says "no" and "wait" to people all
the time. *Why can't I?*

The world moves so fast that I have learned that if I want to
do life at godspeed, I will have to make some people and some
things wait. Why? Because I am waiting on God. He walks
wherever He goes. God can be frustratingly slow. There are even
times when He stops. But if I follow a God who can raise the
dead, I'm never going to be late. More important than the miracle
is what He teaches along the way.

If you want to go far, be careful that you don't go fast. You
can't speed through the things that really matter and think that
you will get very far (Bible reading, meditating on Scripture,
prayer, waiting on God, discernment, speaking life into your
children, nurturing your marriage). Walk at godspeed.

Paths

In all your ways acknowledge him, and he will make straight your paths. -Proverbs 3:6 (ESV)

In his inaugural address, Franklin D. Roosevelt said about America, "We don't know where we are going, but we are on our way."³ Do you know where you are going? You need to know. Why? Because the next step could change everything.

The question of where you are going can be asked of many areas of life. Financially, if you continue with the same spending habits at your current income level, where are you going? How about your family? If you continue parenting as you are, managing your home as you do, how will those decisions impact your children? If your marriage continues as it is, where will it end up? As a student, if you continue applying your current study and work habits, will you achieve your goals? Ultimately, the question needs to be asked of us eternally. If you continue to believe as you do and live as you are, where will you be in eternity? Will it be Heaven or will it be Hell?

There is a big difference between what we hope will happen and what may actually happen. We want life to go well, but there are no guarantees. Yet, I will guarantee you this - you will not end up where you want to be if you don't have a reliable path to get there. Desire is useless if you are not walking the proper path to your chosen destination. Unfortunately, FDR's words ring true in the way we do a lot of things, "We don't know where we are going, but we are on our way."

We need to be sure that we are not going a long way, the wrong way.

I want to introduce two passages into our conversation about paths: Jeremiah 6:16 and Proverbs 3:5-6. I would sum up the general teaching of these two passages in a single statement. *We have a good God who desires for us to end up in a good place, but He has a very deliberate path for us to get there.*

In Jeremiah 6 the prophet proclaims that God wanted to give His people rest. In Proverbs 3 we see God desires to give His people long life (v. 2), favor (v. 4), straight, smooth paths (v. 6), total healing (v. 8), prosperity (v. 10), and His fatherly reproof (v. 12). We could say these things are true for every area of life about which we asked the previous question. Would you like God's favor in your business? Would you like His healing power to mend areas of damage and disease? Long life? This book is all about going a long way. Where are you going?

God desires for there to be peace, favor, and longevity in our families, in our work, in our finances, in our marriage, and in our study. God especially desires for these things to be true of His people eternally. But God doesn't desire to wish these things upon us and send us on our way without knowing where we are going. He has a very defined path. God wants us to walk so that we may obtain these things.

Simply desiring for life to end up in a good place is not enough, there must be a right path. The way we are going determines where we end up. Where we end up has nothing to do with our dreams or desires. There has to be an intentional walk down the path toward your destination.

I know a lot of people who have great wedding pictures but terrible marriages. The ceremony was picture perfect, but the marriage, not so much. At the wedding they had a great photographer, but in the marriage they are walking down the wrong path. When I am asked as a pastor to officiate a wedding, I always ask, "Do you want a great wedding or do you want a great marriage?" You can have both, but most people are only focused on one day in which they will say, "I do" rather than thinking through what that means for the rest of their lives.

With a little planning and nice decorations you can have a great wedding. Weddings are easy. Weddings are well choreographed ceremonies. Marriages are long, drawn out walks. Great marriages require deliberate, directional steps. If you want your marriage, or anything in your life to go far, for that matter . . . if you want all that God has for you, there must be very deliberate, direct steps in the right direction.

Your next step could change everything.

From Jeremiah 6:16 and Proverbs 3:5-6 we can glean two important ideas about paths. 1) We need to evaluate our current path. 2) We must establish our walk on the right path.

Evaluate my current path.

The nation of Israel was at a crossroads in Jeremiah's time. Economically and politically, they were beginning to experience the loss of many of the things God desired for them that we outlined in Proverbs 3. God's favor, prosperity, protection, and guidance were all dwindling away. God also warned them that in the not too distant future they were facing the aggressive attack of a foreign enemy, defeat, and captivity. Yet through His prophet, God offered His people an opportunity to respond to a message that would change their situation. The next step WOULD change everything.

Thus says the LORD: "Stand by the roads, and look, and ask for the ancient paths, where the good way is; and walk in it, and find rest for your souls. But they said, 'We will not walk in it.'" - Jeremiah 6:16 (ESV)

Even when we are on the wrong path, God, in his grace, has a way of interrupting life and giving us an opportunity to change directions. It may be as subtle an interruption as reading a book or a conversation you had with a godly friend. Perhaps there are some things happening in your family or work relationships that signal that there may be difficult days ahead unless something changes. Sadly, sometimes it is tragedy that God somehow uses as a point of grace in our lives that brings us to a crossroads. Whatever the reason, crossroads bring with them critical decisions. In Jeremiah 6:16 God gave His people four directives to help them evaluate their path. He told them to *stand*, *look*, *ask*, and *walk*.

Stand - Honesty

The command to stand is an awakening moment of honesty. Before you take another step, be honest about where you really are. Is it where you thought you would be? Are you in the right place? Are you in a good place? For me, turning 40 caused me to stand. It was a much needed, sobering moment of honesty. Honest moments can be difficult moments. Even so, don't lose sight of this truth: You have a good God who desires for you to end up in a good place.

As I said, standing requires honesty. Three of the most powerful words that can change almost any situation are the simple statement "I was wrong." That statement is painful, but it can take you a long way.

If you want to grab on to all that God desires for you, be willing to stand at the critical crossroads of life God offers you and admit where you were wrong.

Look - Clarity

The call to look is about clarity. You certainly don't want to take another step until you can be honest about what is behind you. But you also don't want to take another step until you can clearly see down the path of the choices that are now before you.

At almost every crossroads there are signs. Some of those signs tell you the names of the roads. Some of the signs may direct you toward desired destinations. Some of the signs are mile markers. Some of the signs are warnings. At some crossroads you are not allowed to make certain turns. Pay attention to the signs.

What do the signs that are around you say? Every choice creates with it a unique set of signs that will show up at the next crossroads. Do the signs in your life tell you that the path you're on is working? Do the signs invite you to change? Are there warning signs? Are there signs that you are enjoying all that God has for you? Are there signs telling you that you are on the right path and that the next step is just a few miles ahead?

One Saturday afternoon my family and I went to downtown Chattanooga. I was driving and we were aimlessly searching through the streets for a new place to eat. Enjoying our conversation and the scenery, I pulled up to a major intersection and saw the oddest thing. The red lights hanging above the intersection were facing backwards. So were the signs on the side walk. The cars parked along the side of the road were all facing the wrong way. I looked at it for a moment and I thought to myself, "Someone has made a huge mistake here!" That someone was me. Somewhere along the way I had missed a very important sign. It was a sign that was obviously behind me - one that read in large black letters "One Way!"

Because I had ignored the sign that said "One Way" every other sign became an indication that I was going the wrong way.

It is hard to admit sometimes that we are the problem. We want to blame everyone else but ourselves. Yet, in His grace God brings us to a crossroads for a moment of honesty and clarity. If you have gone from one relationship to another and each one of them has been a disaster; if you go from job to job and can't find a group of people you can work with; if you go from church to church and you fail to connect or you always find yourself leaving offended; if you find yourself constantly in insurmountable debt; if you find constantly that the signs around you are against you, maybe the someone who has made the huge mistake . . . is you. It is much easier to blame everyone else, but at some point we need to take a look and realize that the fool facing the wrong way on a one way is me.

Ask - Vulnerability

Asking requires vulnerability. Previously I said that three of the most powerful words that can help you change your situation are "I was wrong." Allow me to give you three more that are equally as powerful: "I don't know."

The Christ-based 12-step program *Celebrate Recovery* has a common statement of confession in its first of 12 steps and in its first of 8 principles. It is to admit that I am powerless to control myself, and as a result my life is unmanageable. Week after week in the church I serve as pastor, I witness people who come to a life-changing crossroads and ask for directions.

Men are notorious for not wanting to ask for directions. GPS is nothing but technological camouflage for the male ego. Before GPS, when men failed to reach their destination, they were forced to ask for directions. Yet men held off as long as possible, doing their best to somehow survive being aimlessly lost. Why?

Because for a man, asking for directions from another human being was the ultimate admission of defeat.

Are you willing to ask for directions? Are you willing to listen to what God is saying? Who is speaking into your life? Are you listening to sermons, reading the Bible, or listening to godly counsel? When you do, do you generally think of how those words apply to someone else, or do you receive them as if they are directed toward you?

Jeremiah said to ask for the ancient paths. The expression "ancient paths" refers to how Israel's forefathers gleaned wisdom for life from the Word of God. Our culture has a constant craving for something new. Postmodernism has made us skeptical of anything old and established. We are suckers for the latest show that offers the best advice. Afternoon television is filled with judges, psychics, doctors, panels of women, panels of men, celebrities, and psychiatrists, all promising to offer a topic each day that will change everything for you. As good as it all sounds, we too easily forget that with television, despite the experts they claim to be, the name of the game is not to get you on the right path. The name of the game is to get you to the commercials.

If we want to go further, *we don't need something new as much as we desperately need to be responsive to what God has already said.* We don't need new paths, we need proven ones. We need to do what Jeremiah prophesied to the people - ask for the ancient paths. We need to get back to reading and living the Word of God. A Bible reading plan is no good without a Bible

DOING plan. We need to invite godly people who are further down the road with the Lord than we are to speak counsel into our lives. If you want to go further, be humble enough to ask for directions from people who are already there. Asking the right people the right questions could change your situation.

Walk - Obedience

Once we admit our wrong and find the path that is right, the only mistake we can make at this point is to fail to take the proper turn. What sort of fool gets the right directions but goes a different way? Me! If GPS has proven anything it is that fools drive cars everyday. Too often my device has offered the next step in the journey, and I have actually responded by saying, "That can't be right." You can have all the guidance in the world, but if you don't actually take the turns, those words are wasted and worthless.

Doing what the Bible says can be more of a challenge to the obstinate heart than knowing what the Bible says. God's desire for us is not merely that we know and understand the Word of God, but that we obey it.

This brings us to our next step. Once we evaluate our current path, we need to establish our walk on the right path. Proverbs 3:5-6 shows us how.

Establish my walk on the right path.

Proverbs 3:5-6 says, *"Trust in the LORD with all your heart, and do not lean on your own understanding. In all your ways acknowledge him, and he will make straight your paths."*

In Proverbs 3:5-6 we find two directives that will help us establish our walk on the right path. Each of these directives bring with them an essential qualifier - "all."

You can't do this halfway. To establish your walk on the right path, you must go all the way. The two directives are to 1) trust the Lord with all your heart and to 2) acknowledge Him in all your ways.

Trust the Lord with all your heart.

The word *trust* raises an immediate red flag. In a culture that has become so untrustworthy it is hard not to have some degree of trust issues. We have been made a fool before. Why fail and be made a fool again? Within my audience of readers and listeners there are a myriad of stories of failed trust. From bad business deals to failed marriages, from abusive parents to abusive churches, from failed love to failed loans, I am certain we can all offer reasons why it is difficult for us to trust anyone or anything.

If trust is not hard enough, the author of the proverb closes the loophole. You must trust the Lord with all your heart. When our trust is broken, a sense of shame enters us emotionally. The usual response is to harden the heart just a bit as a defense mechanism. We withhold trust and create a barrier to the heart that must be hurdled by the next more highly qualified emotional acrobat if trust is ever to be offered again. That wall to the heart is much higher and harder in some than it is in others. With every hurt we add a layer of brick.

The Hebrew word translated "trust," used in Proverbs 3:5, is interesting. Most often "trust" in the Bible is used to describe things you can't trust.[4] You can't trust wealth or the world. You can't trust others. You can't even trust yourself. Isn't it ironic that the Bible made a long list of things you can't trust long before you did?

So there is your trust, torn and tattered . . . somewhere locked away with your heart behind a massive wall of brick built out of things you said you would never do again. And here you are at a crossroads, ready to establish a new path, and the Lord says before we can take the next life-changing step, "I need to see your trust with all your heart."

It's like getting pulled over at a road block and the state trooper asking to see your registration and proof of insurance. I am not a very organized person. In that moment, he might as well ask me to pull a unicorn out of my glovebox.

So here we go fumbling through the mess of it all. Uncomfortably we say, "I know it's in here somewhere." Mmm, hmm, right beside the unicorn. We are hoping that in the sincerity of our search, the trooper will give us the benefit of the doubt that we really do have an insurance card, registration, and a unicorn and let us go on our merry way. This has worked for me more times than I can count. But with God, He just keeps standing there, waiting until we pull out the proverbial unicorn.

So if and when we finally dig it out and produce it, we can tell our heart and our trust have been hopelessly buried for quite a while. Years of damaged goods and hurtful stories are piled on top of it. Here is the incredible thing about the word "trust" as it is translated in Proverbs 3:5: The trust that we gave to all the wrong things is the same trust God wants. He is not looking for a theologically robust trust. All He asks is for what is there, expired, damaged, and buried. But whatever it is, He requires ALL that is left.

Remember, we serve a good God who desires for us to end up in a good place. With every step down the right path the Lord will foster with the experiences a growing and deepening trust. We will talk about this more in a later chapter entitled "Presence." But trust is built with the Lord the longer you walk with Him and realize that He will not leave you or forsake you. You can walk a long way down the path of restoring trust.

Acknowledge Him in all your ways.

We must not only trust God wholeheartedly; to walk with Him on the right path means also that we must look to Him for everything. The word "acknowledge" comes from a common Hebrew Word that is usually translated, "to know or to learn." To acknowledge the Lord in all your ways means to learn from Him about everything.[5]

How much further could you go if you slowed down and sought the Lord's counsel before you made decisions? Remember one of the benefits of walking with God? Those who walk with God are able to make critical decisions at key moments and accomplish incredible things. Why? Because they acknowledge the Lord in all their ways.

To "trust the Lord with all your heart" and to "acknowledge Him in all your ways" stands in contrast to the idea "and lean not on your own understanding." The Bible says in Proverbs 14:12, *"There is a way that seems right to a man, but its end is the way to death."* Trusting the Lord with all our heart and acknowledging Him in all our ways is at first disorienting, because we have never navigated our paths like this. There will be times in the path where the Lord's leading may seem counterintuitive to the choices we would have otherwise made for ourselves. Even still, leaning on our own understanding can be dangerous.

My wife Shannon refers to me as the human GPS. Other than going the wrong way down a one way street, my sense of direction is otherwise reliable. I have successfully navigated our way down unfamiliar paths numerous times. Most of the time I can tell you what direction we need to go to end up where we want to be. There is something about me that even likes getting lost just so I can prove to everyone in the car that I can get us on the right path again. That's sick, I know. While I may regard my sense of direction as remarkable, I promise you it is not flawless.

Not long after we moved to Birmingham, Alabama in 2002 to serve at Ridgecrest Baptist Church, my wife and I became good friends with two couples in the congregation who had daughters nearly the same age as our own. The husbands in the respective families also served in our church as deacons. From time to time we would take trips together. If it was a trip for several days, the tradition was that one day would be ladies' day, and all the dads would keep the kids. The following day would be MAN day, and all the moms would, in turn, watch the kids. On this particular trip we were in Pigeon Forge, Tennessee, a tourist trap full of hotels and overpriced shows nestled in the Smoky Mountains. On MAN day I determined we were going to escape the trappings of touristville and we were going to MAN up with a hike in the mountains.

There was a particular place, called Elkmont, high up in the mountains, where we frequently camped when I was a child. I knew of an old home place hidden in the forest where a legendary mountain man once lived, so I drove the guys deep into the woods to see it. Once we arrived and explored a bit, we found a trail. After a brief conversation we all agreed that this would be the trail we would hike. Off we went into the forest. The problem is that we proceeded down the trail more like three men who had just paid $150 for a dinner show the night before than we did like three men who knew how to survive in the wilderness. We had no map, no food, no water, and no compass. Perfect.

After a couple of hours of walking we stopped to assess our situation. The sun was still high in the sky, but, being deep in the forest, we knew once it began to set, it would get dark quickly. My friend Allen offered the group some sage advice: "All I know is that if we turn around and go back the way we came, we will end up where we started."

Yet I, the human GPS, had another perspective. "Guys, I have been watching this hillside since we started walking, and it has stayed on our left the entire time. It seems to me like we are walking around it. I saw another trailhead just below the one we entered. I think this is a loop. What if we turn around now and walk back? If we turn around, we may double our distance when we might be near the end."

By that time I estimated we had walked 2.5 miles. Why walk 2.5 more when we may be only a few hundred yards from the end? Sounds logical, right? For some reason, they agreed and so on we walked down the path.

As the shadows grew longer, the conversation continued. Allen: "All I know is that if we turn around and go back the way we came . . ." Me: "I have been watching this hillside . . . I think this is a loop." Each time I reasoned that if we turn back we may double our distance.

After actually doubling our distance, for some reason my now former friends, but fellow hikers continued to believe me.

Several miles later the shadows had turned into a mild cover of darkness. Allen had offered us a grand opportunity: Turn back. But that offer had long since passed and we were now so far down the trail - tired, thirsty, hungry, and ill equipped - that by this time turning back meant walking back in the dark.

Just after we began talking about how to survive the night we came to a crossroads in the path. The sign pointed, 5 miles to a pump station in the direction of Cades Cove, 3 miles to Metcalf

Bottoms. I had been to the Smoky Mountains enough to know three things about Metcalf Bottoms. One, it was indeed the bottom as the name indicates. A nice descent would be welcome at this point. Two, the main road runs alongside the creek at Metcalf Bottoms. Perhaps we could be rescued. Three, Metcalf Bottoms was a long, long way from where we started - twelve miles by car to be exact. You may ask how I would know that? Allow me to explain.

When we three men emerged from the ever darkening wood, dirty and haggard, we were forced to do something I had never previously experienced. The preacher who had turned MAN day into an almost disastrous hike would now have to resort to hiking of another sort: hitch-hiking. So there we stood at the edge of the road. Three dirty, dorky men, flagging down cars in the curve.

Finally, a kind elderly couple from Michigan pulled over to the side of the road. I had already rehearsed what I would say in my mind several times. "Sir, ma'am. My name is Brian. I am a pastor in Birmingham, Alabama. These men are two of my deacons. We are lost in the woods and we need a ride back to our car." That's right, a twelve-mile ride.

Lean not on your own understanding! There is a way that seems right to a man, but the end thereof is a very dark hike! God is not like a foolish preacher who thinks he is a human GPS. God really does know where He is going. He wants you to go a long way, the right way. He is good, and He will lead you to a good place if you will trust Him with all your heart and acknowledge Him in all your ways to establish for you the right path.

The Proverb says, depending on the translation you read, that God will direct or straighten your path. This means He will make it right. He will smooth it out. In ancient times straight roads were good roads. "Straight" did not merely speak of the absence of twists and turns, but also of the absence of obstacles in the way. If this is the case, how do we then reconcile the times when we do follow the Lord down the right path but the way is not straight, but extremely difficult?

One of the key themes of the wisdom books in the Bible (Job, Psalms, Proverbs, and Ecclesiastes) is the suffering of the righteous and the prosperity of the wicked. Why is it that at times God's people seem to suffer greatly while godless people do quite well?

To answer this question, you have to look down the path. The world may seem curvy and out of sorts currently, but there is coming a day when the Lord will straighten the paths. When He does so, those who walk with Him will be the only ones left to eternally enjoy the good destination to which God brings them. Later in Proverbs 3, the father speaking the proverb says to his son, "*My son, do not lose sight of these-keep sound wisdom and discretion, and they will be life for your soul and adornment for your neck. Then you will walk on your way securely, and your foot will not stumble . . .Do not be afraid of sudden terror or of the ruin of the wicked when it comes, for the LORD will be your confidence and will keep your foot from being caught." - Proverbs 3:21-23, 25-26 (ESV)*

He goes on to say in verses 33-35, *"The LORD's curse is on the house of the wicked, but he blesses the dwelling of the righteous. Toward the scorners he is scornful, but to the humble he gives favor. The wise will inherit honor, but fools get disgrace."*

Paths lead to destinations. The Bible is clear in its teaching that the path of following Christ to eternal life begins difficult but ends in salvation. Jesus teaches this in Matthew 7:13-14: *"Enter by the narrow gate. For the gate is wide and the way is easy that leads to destruction, and those who enter by it are many. For the gate is narrow and the way is hard that leads to life, and those who find it are few."* When it comes to the right path, we need to be able to see the immediate, but we especially need to see ultimate. Where does it lead?

Sadly, Jeremiah records the reply of the people to God's gracious offer of rest for their souls. A good God, who wants to lead His people to a good place, invites them to Stand, Look, Ask, and Walk. And their reply: *"But they said, 'We will not walk in it.'"* *- Jeremiah 6:16c (ESV)*

We will live with the consequences of our path. People who establish the right path and walk with God are able to see the ultimate and realize that the immediate is not permanent. They are not looking fast, they are looking far. We trust that God will, in His time, uphold His promises and the path will end up straight, in the right place.

The Bible offers us the stories of the outcomes of several chosen paths. For Abraham, walking with God meant leaving everything that was familiar. Even though he stumbled at times, God led him to his chosen destination. An old man with an infertile wife long past child-bearing years, miraculously conceived a child as God resurrected a twice-dead womb (Gen. 18:11). Abraham became the father of a great nation and the great-grandfather of our salvation.

Moses chose to walk with God. When God led him to the Red Sea, God uncovered a flooded path by parting the waters, and the people who followed Him walked through on dry ground. God straightened Moses' path.

Joshua was a warrior. In his path to his destiny stood Jericho, with its insurmountable walls. God told the mighty warrior to do the strangest thing: Use no weaponry, only walk. On the seventh day the walls fell down flat. God straightened Joshua's path.

There are other stories in the Bible of poor choices of paths that led to undesirable locations. Adam and Eve walked a path of exile out of the garden. Because the first generation of slaves rescued from Egypt complained and did not trust the Lord, they were left to wander in the wilderness, a 40 year death march to destruction. As we read the words of Jesus in Matthew 7 just a few paragraphs ago, we each have a path to choose: a broad way and a narrow one. The broad way, Jesus says, leads to destruction, and there are many who find it.

What will be your choice? *Stand. Look. Ask. Walk.* Trust the Lord - with ALL your heart. Acknowledge Him - in ALL your ways. He will make your paths straight. Don't trade your destiny for destruction by choosing the wrong path. If you desire to go further, make this moment a crossroad and choose wisely.

Presence

You make known to me the path of life; in your presence there is fullness of joy; at your right hand are pleasures forevermore. - Psalm 16:11 (ESV)

The *Oxford Dictionary* deemed the word "selfie" as the word of the year in 2013. Research showed its frequency of use in the English language had soared more than 17,000% in 12 months. A selfie is a photo you take of yourself using your smart phone. It is essentially a picture of your face at arm's length.

Selfies have become a cultural craze. President Obama was criticized for taking several selfies at Nelson Mandella's funeral. Major athletes and pop stars frequently post selfies. The Pope even poses frequently in crowds for those who want selfies. Selfies are such a cultural phenomenon that Sunday has been unofficially declared "Selfie Sunday."

Recently a news story surfaced in the British paper *The Mirror* reporting that Danny Bowman, a 19-year-old British man, spent 10 hours a day taking up to 200 pictures of himself on his phone, trying feverishly to get the shot right before he would dare to even post one. The teenager became so obsessed with taking the perfect selfie, he tried to kill himself when he failed to do so.

He dropped out of school. Bowman didn't leave his house for six months and lost 28 pounds trying to make himself look better for the camera. "The normally temperate boy became extremely aggressive with his parents when they tried to confiscate his phone and curb his obsessive behavior."

The psychologist that treated Danny says that even though his patient is an extreme case, selfie addiction is widespread and is now recognized as a mental illness.[6]

The recent phenomenon with selfies on *Instagram* and other social media sites makes the current version a much easier target, but every generation has its own version of the selfie. However you snap it, with your mind or your smartphone, a selfie is the ideal picture of yourself, one that garners the admiration and approval of others.

I don't know what your ideal selfie is, your ideal version of life, but there is a frustration with it all, that, on a deeper level, we can share with Danny Bowman. No matter how many times we try to get a shot of the perfect version of self, we never can quite get it right.

The word "presence" in the Old Testament is most often an English translation of the Hebrew word "face." The Bible often talks about being in the presence of God, or before His face.

God has a selfie.

God has invited man to do an interesting thing with his life, to walk before Him or to literally be in His face. In Genesis 17:1 God invited Abraham to live before his face: "*When Abram was ninety-nine years old the LORD appeared to Abram and said to him, 'I am God Almighty; walk before me, and be blameless.'*"

Solomon prayed to the Lord and cited God's promise to honor David's legacy of establishing the throne of his son who would walk before God's face: *"Now therefore, O LORD, God of Israel, keep for your servant David my father what you have promised him, saying, 'You shall not lack a man to sit before me on the throne of Israel, if only your sons pay close attention to their way, to walk before me as you have walked before me."* - 1 Kings 8:25 (ESV)

When it comes to selfies, we don't need the right picture of our face, but of God's face.

This sounds strange to us - to think in terms of living life before God's face, always in His presence, to be enamored with His selfie above all others. The reason we struggle with this idea is because we resist any attempt to make life about anyone else but ourselves. We come by this struggle honestly. As I pointed out in the opening chapter, after we sinned, the Bible says of Adam and the woman, *"And they heard the sound of the LORD God walking in the garden in the cool of the day, and the man and his wife **hid themselves from the presence** of the LORD God among the trees of the garden."* - Genesis 3:8 (ESV)

The man and the woman hid themselves from God's face.

Since the moment we ate the fruit from the tree of the knowledge of good and evil, we have been engaged in a desperate attempt to take the glory that was meant for God's face and direct it toward our own. We want some version of self that everyone admires, that is satisfying and forever fulfilling. Like Danny

Bowman, we take that arm's length snapshot of life over and over again, but it never pans out to be what we thought it should be. So we try again and again, in a desperate search for that one perfect picture.

Inherent in the selfie is some form of egotistical idolatry.[7] In the world of social media people post their selfie and then try to garner "likes." "Likes" are digital clicks that become quantifiable expressions of approval.[8] For teenagers this has become a cruel obsession.

Danny Bowman, the kid addicted to selfies, explained the impact of the likes and comments like this: "People would comment on them, but children can be cruel. One told me my nose was too big for my face and another picked on my skin. I started taking more and more to try to get the approval of my friends. I would be so high when someone wrote something nice but gutted when they wrote something unkind."[9]

When we offer our souls on the altar of public approval, we are as equally close to being self-absorbed as we are to being "gutted." Idolatry never ends well.

In Psalm 16:11, the Psalmist does something unusual. Instead of garnering attention to his own face, he focuses his attention on God's face and finds the most incredible thing.

"You make known to me the path of life; in your presence there is fulness of joy; at your right hand are pleasures forevermore."

Think about it like this. When we post something to social media we hope that the end result is that it will be "trending."

"Trending" means that it is setting a new standard. It is capturing cultural admiration. It is what's "next." According to the Psalmist, he found in God's face something that is always trending. "You make known to me the path of life." Those who walk with God walk with someone who knows what's next.

Danny Bowman was never satisfied with his selfie, but the Psalmist found in God's face total satisfaction. He describes it as "fulness of joy."

When we place our worth in the approval of others, we will find no consistency. As I said previously, you are either self-absorbed, inflated by a false sense of approval, or gutted by criticism and rejection. In the Lord, the Psalmist found consistent pleasure that he described as "forevermore." Nothing is capable of gutting the pleasure we find before God's face.

Why is it that when we turn our attention to God's face instead of our own, we are more prone to be satisfied? Before I answer that question, I think there is a caveat in all of this that needs to be addressed.

I have a very perceptive teenage daughter. When I shared with her my thoughts on this topic, she asked a great question. *If we are selfish in trying to garner the approval and admiration of others for ourselves, isn't God just as selfish as we are if He wants all of our attention to be upon Him?* If God puts forth His face and invites us to walk before Him, isn't He just as deranged and idolatrous as we?

Allow me to answer a question with a question. *If God is perfect and in Him is knowledge of the path of life, fulness of joy, and pleasure forevermore, is God selfish in inviting us to experience Him, or is He generous?*

Obviously, He is generous. We could even say that He is more than generous because we are certainly undeserving of such an incredible gift.

Let's flip that question around. *If we know there is no version of self that we can produce that brings complete satisfaction and lasting pleasure, are we innocent in trying to capture the perfect selfie . . . or insane?*

Exactly.

Now let's answer the main question on the table. When you turn your attention from your face to focusing on God's, why is it that you are more likely to be satisfied? The reason is because when you focus your attention on living life before God's face *you only need one "like."*

John Piper says it like this: "God is most glorified in us when we are most satisfied in Him."

Walking in God's presence turns life upside down. What we once thought critical becomes incomparable to the wisdom for life, fullness of joy, and everlasting pleasure we find in Him. Long walks in God's presence give us proper perspective. Going far takes focus. People who go far understand what is most important.

Before you sacrifice your soul for a version of self that cannot possibly deliver, compare it to what the Psalmist found in God's presence by asking three questions: Is it trending? Is it satisfying? Is it lasting?

Is it trending?

Social media calls them "trends." Sociologists call them "memes." "Memes" are the interesting mannerisms, phrases, and fashions that seem for a time to become cultural DNA. You've probably called them "fads." No one quite knows how or why, but all of the sudden everybody's got one or everybody's doing it.

For a short time there was "planking", these strange photos that surfaced of people lying rigid on common, everyday things like water fountains, poles, pianos, or cars. Then there was "Gangham style." Who would have ever thought such a dumb dance on a low budget video by a nerdy dude rapping lyrics in Korean would take America by storm.

Next was the "Harlem Shake." From football teams to office staffs, everyone set up a camera and filmed themselves going about their mundane tasks. Everyone in the scene looks bored but one. It is as if he is dancing to a rhythm no one hears but him. Suddenly the scene changes. With some creative editing, the beat hits and everyone on screen goes nuts.

Currently, it seems that every girl on *Instagram* has to stand Kardashian style at a perfect angle with hand on hip. They say that putting your hand on your hip is slimming. I had no idea that a hand had so much potential.

Something must be wrong with my hand.

And this thing with Grumpy cat - where in the world does it come from? Who knows, but you will see him in the most unexpected places. These things come and go; before long it will be something else that captures the culture and trends.

When the Psalmist turned his attention toward God's face, he found that, "*You make known to me the path of life.*" Can you imagine walking through life with someone greater and wiser than you, who knows what is coming next? What an incredible opportunity for those who want to go further, to know what's next. The Psalmist says in Psalm 116:8-8, "*For you have delivered my soul from death, my eyes from tears, my feet from stumbling; I will walk before the LORD in the land of the living.*"

When it comes to difficulty, God's Word and His Spirit can help us either prevent it or endure it. Many people misunderstand the prophetic gift that God gives His people. They think of prophecy as foretelling, as in being able to predict something otherwise unforeseen. While prophecy certainly does contain a degree of this in the Bible, most of what we see in prophecy is really "forth"-telling. Forth-telling is the uncanny ability to know how God's world works. It is the ability to declare common sense consequence rather than reveal something unpredictable. Forth-telling is alerting others to something that should be clearly seen. Prophecy is predicting a future consequence based on truth. If you put your hand in a flame, you will be burned. Prophetic!

Much of the preaching of the Old Testament prophets is based on what God had said long ago in the Book of Deuteronomy. There, God set before His people a choice - blessing or cursing. If they followed the Lord, it would result in blessing for their lives. If they disobeyed His Word, the end result would be curse. As the Old Testament narrative plays out, this is certainly the case. As the people walked away from God's Word, the prophets would arrive and begin reminding them of what God had said. Not surprisingly, their future went just as God ordained, based on their choices.

We should be no less surprised that when we disobey God's Word, we pay a price. No one is immune from consequences.

Prophecy was not all about cursing. It was also the prediction of blessing as the consequence of obedience. If the people obeyed the Lord, the prophets "forth"-told of the blessings that awaited them.

In social media there is another interesting word to describe things that are trending. It is the word "viral." When a video goes "viral" it means that people are sharing it and that it is popping up on computers everywhere. It becomes socially contagious, sort of like a virus. *God is not only capable of preparing us for what's next, but He is also capable of setting our feet on paths that will unleash viral blessings in our life.*

In Ephesians 2:8-10 Paul makes a powerful statement about those who are saved. He says, "*For by grace you have been saved through faith. And this is not your own doing; it is the gift of God, not a result of works, so that no one may boast. For we are his workmanship, created in Christ Jesus for good works, which God prepared beforehand, that we should walk in them.*"

Being saved is not simply about escaping Hell by receiving eternal life in Jesus Christ. While rescue from Hell is certainly a grand benefit, salvation does not benefit us only in eternity, it benefits us immediately. The call to Christ is a call to a prepared path. According to Ephesians 2:8-10, the redeemed are the walking masterpieces of God. They are on a path of life laid out before them, definitely called for good works, blessings instead of curses.

The choice to obey the Lord and participate in the good works on the path of life unleashes viral blessings. In every action, there is a reaction. You may feel as if there is currently a lot going wrong in your world. For too long you have walked away from God and, instead of viral blessing, you are experiencing viral curse. How can you possibly get life back under control? Walk in the right direction one step at a time. Look at Ephesians 2:8-10, work the plan God has for you.

As we saw in the previous chapter, one step in the right direction can change everything. You may not be able to fix everything immediately, but you may be able to take one step and begin working good in one thing. That one thing may begin to impact a few things, and those few things then begin to change the attitudes and actions of several things. Blessings become viral.

God's Word is instructive for every area of life. Work the plan. If your family is in chaos and your marriage is falling apart, there is something powerful about a husband and a dad who begins to lead based on God's Word. His faith becomes viral in his family. If you feel like your parents are always on your case, there is something powerful about respect, honor, and obedience that begin to change the tension in the situation. If you have an employer that causes you immense pressure and grief, there is something powerful about being godly that can change the tone of your workplace (Ephesians 5:22 - 6:9).

While this may be a good path, it does not guarantee that everything that happens on it is good. We live in a sin-cursed world, and we live in a time in which there are some things God's people can't prevent, but God's people can endure. The Word of God provides us with a powerful foundation that is able to withstand the storms of life and the coming storms of God's judgment (Matthew 7:24-27).

God's people will experience loss and hardship like everyone else, but they will not be destroyed by it. In Psalm 23:4 the Psalmist expresses a calm that is counter cultural to the extreme swings of emotion and panic we see in our society. He says, "Even though I walk through the valley of the shadow of death, I will fear no evil, for you are with me; your rod and your staff, they comfort me." David noticed a trend in His life. God is ever present. He experienced in the midst of his most difficult moments a viral blessing, fear is replaced with comfort.

There is nothing we can give our attention to or invest our lives in that is comparable to the trends that walking before the face of God can unleash in your life. When we live life in God's presence, we need only one "like." God, do you like this decision? God, do you like what I am doing? God, do you like where this is headed? You make known to me the trends, the path of life. You can go a long way on what God likes.

Is it satisfying?

It is difficult for many of us to believe that God wants us to be satisfied. My wife affectionately refers to me sometimes as a "fun-sucker." A "fun-sucker" is someone who can emotionally vaporize every ounce of joy in a room with a single word. I am a master at the craft.

One of our favorite things to do in the spring of the year is to attend the University of Georgia G-Day football game. The weather is warming. There is a real family atmosphere in the stadium. It has been a long, dark winter and it has been a long time since we have seen some football. Best of all, its free! A game will cost my family a small fortune in the fall, but the spring game is perfectly priced.

We get out of bed the morning of G-Day and the weather is perfect. Our plan is to stop at a mom-and-pop breakfast joint in our town and grab biscuits on the way to the game. Apparently, everyone else in the metropolis of Chatsworth, Georgia had the same plan. We live in a small town with only a few thousand people. Apparently all of them meet up at the same hole-in-the wall joint for biscuits and invite out-of-town guests.

We sat at the drive-thru 5 minutes, 10 minutes, 20 minutes, and it seemed like we had moved less than a car length closer to the window. It was at that moment that fun sucker determined to save the day.

I loudly expressed to every passenger in my van my thoughts regarding the inefficiency of the restaurant servers. I condemned harshly the idea that other people in our town would want biscuits as badly as I did. Comparatively, I pointed out why my day must certainly be more important than theirs. How dare the good people of Chatsworth inconvenience a man on a schedule going to a glorified spring football practice! By the time I had yelled, stomped, and slung gravel while bolting out of the parking lot, there was not a single ounce of fun left within the confines of our Honda Odyssey van. Mission accomplished.

For some reason we believe God is a "fun-sucker." We believe God is a mostly stoic, otherwise temperamental, unpredictable, ruler of the universe who requires us to be miserable if we are to have any shot at being godly. If you share this belief allow me to ask a few questions.

Who was it that created the Garden of Eden full of perfect provision and told Adam and the Eve to have it all, but one?

Who was it that invented the day off?

Who was it that instituted seven feast days on the Jewish calendar?

Who was it that created the concept of a promised land flowing with milk and honey?

Who created Paradise?

God is not a fun-sucker. The God of the Bible is happy.

In John 17 we have recorded a divine conversation between Jesus and the Father. There Jesus prays, "But now I am coming to you, and these things I speak in the world, that *they may have my joy fulfilled in themselves.*" - John 17:13 (ESV)

Have you ever thought about the fact that if there is to be any possibility of happiness in the world, then the creator of the world must be happy?[10] God is infinitely happy.

As a happy God, the Bible teaches that there are things that God approves, that He delights in (Psalm 35:27). We have a God who actually likes things. Remember why we said that, when we turn our attention to God's face instead of our own, we are more likely to be satisfied? Because you need only one "like."

Someone may object and point quickly to the Ten Commandments. It is difficult to envision a happy God who likes anything when the 10 most familiar statements in the Bible begin "Thou shalt not." Through our eyes we see God as a warden on patrol. He has a scowl on His face and He is quick to bring harsh judgment on anyone who dares to break one of the ten rules. But is that really a fair assessment of what the Ten Commandments truly are?

Is it really fair to presume that negative statements are always motivated by hate? When a child walks too close to a fire, is it hateful for a mother to scream out, "Stop!" Is it judgmental for the manufacturers of rat poison to put a skull and crossbones on the box and to warn you that, if you eat it, you will die? Think about this: Do the warnings on a box of poison diminish in any way the pleasure that is found in cake?

What we need on a box of poison is a warning about the contents, not a commentary on the taste of cake. Would you rather the box list all the things you can eat and allow you to figure out by the process of elimination what you can't eat without harmful repercussions? No way! What we need is for warnings to get to the point. It's not so much negative as it is practical.

What if you rethought the Ten Commandments and didn't see them only as negative statements, but as affirmations of what God loves? If the Ten Commandments are the primary list for what God doesn't like, what do the Ten say about what God does like?

Let's take the last 6 as an example. The last 6 govern our relationships with one another. Honor your father and your mother. Why, because God loves the family.

You shall not murder. God loves life.

You shall not commit adultery. God loves loving marriages built on trust.

You shall not steal. God wants you to enjoy ownership and have security with your stuff.

You shall not bear false witness. God loves truth and in the same way He protects His image (no graven images, do not take the Lord's name in vain), He protects your reputation.

You shall not covet your neighbor's house or wife . . . or anything that is your neighbor's. God values contentment and security in community.

Is it really a fun-sucker move on God's part to protect your property, your marriage, your parents, your children, and your very life? The Ten Commandments say more about who God is and what God likes than they do about what He doesn't.

If you will learn to like what God likes, you can have your fill of it. It is here that the word "fun-sucker" enters the equation. So what does God like? Is it singing in the choir? Wow, now that sounds eternally fun - forever a choir boy!

Surely God likes modesty. Does that mean I must wear khaki and white everyday? If we like what God likes, we imagine ourselves having only our fill of a monkish life, holed up in a bell tower, hooked on Gregorian chants, destined to forever wear khaki. Nothing could be further from the truth. God has greater desires than khaki for His people.

Think about this, if it satisfies the Lord, how could it not possibly satisfy you? If an infinitely happy God likes it, you'll love it! In his book *The Weight of Glory*, C.S. Lewis says,

> *Indeed, if we consider the unblushing promises of reward and the staggering nature of the rewards promised in the Gospels, it would seem that Our Lord finds our desires, not too strong, but*

too weak. We are half-hearted creatures, fooling about with drink and sex and ambition when infinite joy is offered us, like an ignorant child who wants to go on making mud pies in a slum because he cannot imagine what is meant by the offer of a holiday at the sea. We are far too easily pleased.[11]

I once shared a message entitled, "Is God Better than Chocolate?" with my congregation. Obviously, I borrowed the title from a common cultural misconception that there is really only one thing in life better than chocolate, and that one thing is sex. I challenged the idea that the commands God uses to hem up our lives, especially those pertaining to sex, cannot possibly bring more pleasure to life than if we were able to go through life unrestrained in our appetites, sexual ones or otherwise. I used C.S. Lewis' quote in the sermon.

As an illustration, I put a table in front of the crowd and upon it were several types of food beneath a cloth. I found a hungry soul in the audience and I told him he could eat as much as he wanted of what I had; the only stipulation was that he had to eat something of everything I offered him. So we proceeded.

Biscuits. It was early in the morning. Who doesn't want a biscuit? Sausage. Again, who would deny sausage? I offered him drinks, candy, and, yes, even chocolate. After the chocolate one thing remained. Baby food. Peas and carrots, I think it was. But my participant was a good sport about it. He reluctantly, but dutifully, downed a heaping spoon of it as agreed; much to the disgust of the crowd. His face also expressed his opinion of the food. He was more than fine with chocolate, not so much with soupy peas and carrots.

Then I asked him. "Of all of these things on the table, which would you like to have more of? Remember, you can have as much as you want." It will be no surprise to you what he said. He wanted more of everything except the baby food.

You may not remember it, but there was a time early on in your life - sometime between formula and teeth - when you thought baby food was "the bomb." Why? At the time, you didn't know what a biscuit was. At the time, you had never tasted chocolate. The only thing your tastebuds were telling you was that baby food was an upgrade from formula, and you were satisfied. Why, because you had no idea that there was so much more out there that tasted so much better.

My mom always said to me as a kid, "You can't say you don't like it if you don't try it." The Psalmist said that when he flipped life upside down and turned all of His attention to living life in God's presence, he found "fullness of joy."

Have you ever really tried living in obedience to God's Word? Try it, you will like it. Remember, you need only one "like."

Is it lasting?

The Psalmist said that when he reversed his focus and began to live life in God's presence, he found *"at your right hand are pleasures forevermore."* When we put the objects of our earthly affections to this final test, do they last? We find that the result is consistent: across-the-board failure. There are some incredible things in this world that bring intense pleasure, but it never lasts. If we look back at our selfies, we will probably find that we overestimated the value of things that ultimately don't matter and grossly underestimated the value of things that eternally do.

Ultimately, there is only one thing that matters. Have you repented of sin and received the gift of eternal life that is in Jesus Christ our Lord? The Psalmist's statement that "at your right hand are pleasures forevermore" is ultimately and eternally fulfilled in Christ alone. In the preceding verse, Psalm 16:10, the writer speaks of the greatest threat of eternal pleasure, and that is the seeming finality of life and corruption of joy that is in death. Yet the Psalmist found, *"For you will not abandon my soul to Sheol, or let your holy one see corruption."*

That statement was ultimately secured in Jesus' death and resurrection. Peter quotes Psalm 16:10-11 on the Day of Pentecost in his sermon recorded in Acts 2. Peter, inspired by the Spirit of God, implores the listening crowd to make no mistake that this everlasting pleasure and victory over death was found in Christ. Peter then ends his sermon with a statement that cut the crowd to the heart. *"Let all the house of Israel therefore know for certain that God has made him both Lord and Christ, this Jesus whom you crucified." - Acts 2:36 (ESV)*

Even though the cross was essential to our salvation, it was at its heart, the ultimate act of human rebellion to murder the Son of God. In Jesus, the people had an invitation to everlasting pleasure. At the cross, they flatly rejected God's offer.

The prophet Isaiah made a chilling observation about the attitude of God's people in His presence:

I was ready to be sought by those who did not ask for me;
I was ready to be found by those who did not seek me.
I said, "Here I am, here I am,"
to a nation that was not called by my name.
I spread out my hands all the day
to a rebellious people,
who walk in a way that is not good,
following their own devices;
a people who provoke me
to my face continually, *- Isaiah 65:1-3 (ESV)*

For those who walk before God's face, they will find pleasure forevermore. We have an incredible invitation. Yet, according to Isaiah, it is like God posts His selfie for all to see and says, "Here I am, Here I am." Why? Because we "walk in a way that is not good, following *our own* devices." Instead of living life before God's face, all we want is for the attention to be drawn to our face.

Look at me.

Admire me.

Like me.

Follow me.

God calls our egotistical idolatry, whatever version of self to which we aspire, something that provokes Him to His face continually. It is the ultimate tragedy.

If you put your soul, your dream, your image on the altar of public approval, the world will kill your selfie. Being first will not get you far. But if you flip life around and live in the presence of God, you need only one "like." If you take every area of your life and post it only for one, there is incredible power in that one "like."

God, do you like the direction of my life? What's next?

God, do you like the things I like? If not, show me what is better. If you like it, I'll love it.

God, do you like the things I'm taking pleasure in?

Walking with God leads us to enjoy what He likes. One "like" will take us a long way.

Providence

The steps of a man are established by the LORD, when he delights in his way; though he fall, he shall not be cast headlong, for the LORD upholds his hand. - Psalm 37:23-24 (ESV)

In the opening chapter I mentioned characteristics of people who walk with God. I mentioned that people who walk with God please the Lord. There is a great reward for people who walk with God. Walking with God describes the way someone does life. It is not just a concept that they apply to some things, like the metaphor of *walking* suggests, it describes the way they do everything.

I also mentioned that our walk was ruined by sin which has caused us to hide from God rather than walk openly with Him. Those who walk with God have had this relationship restored through repentance and faith in Jesus Christ. People who walk with God have come out of hiding and are unashamed that they live for Him.

Another characteristic I mentioned is that people who walk with God are able to make critical decisions at key moments and accomplish incredible things. We see this in Genesis 6:9 with Noah. Because he walked with God, the news of the coming flood was revealed to him, as well as instruction on how to save his family through the building of an ark. In 1 Kings 3, Solomon reflected on his father's walk before the Lord. David's reign as king was characterized by the guidance God gave him to make sound economic decisions, to conquer his enemies, and to prosper his people.

What if you could know the next step? What if you could move through life less reactionary and more strategic? What if life was less of a guess and more of a calculation? Knowing the next step with certainty will help you make decisions that will position you for maximum impact.

Psalm 37:23 says, "*The steps of a man are established by the LORD, when he delights in his way.*"

Notice that the verse doesn't say big days are established by the Lord. God is not an event coordinator.

The verse doesn't say major decisions are established by the Lord. God is not a consultant for hire.

The verse doesn't say the steps of major players are established by the Lord. God isn't an agent for hire.

The Lord establishes steps. He is a pedestrian God. He is a God of the walkers who want to go further.

Have you ever thought about the importance of one step? Probably not. Very few of us have deep thoughts about putting one foot in front of the other . . . at least not until something bad happens. Think about this:

A minor misstep could become a huge mistake.

When we think of marathons, we think of a race of more than 26 miles. As long of a race as a marathon may be, one misstep can reduce a finely tuned athlete into a writhing heap of flesh. There are hundreds of thousands of steps in a marathon. All of them help the runner finish the race. Any one of them could end it.

In the 2008 Beijing Olympics, Jamaican sprinter Usain Bolt broke the world record for 100 meters by .03 seconds. By the time he reached the finish line, he had obliterated the other competitors in the race. What made the difference? Every other sprinter took 44 steps. Bolt finished the course by taking only 41. Steps may seem mundane, but each one of them can make a big difference.

I would surmise that there are steps, decisions you made in your past, that you didn't think were of any real consequence at the time. Now, looking back, you realize that step was a big mistake. Perhaps it slowed you down. Perhaps it crippled you.

I have a friend who lives in Hawaii. On a hike down a remote trail with her family, April took a misstep that resulted in her breaking her ankle. She had to be rescued by helicopter. Later that day the video of her rescuers pulling her out of the jungle was available for the entire world to see on *Yahoo* news. One step and April's fall went viral! She was a good sport about it. Once I knew she was going to recover, I had to laugh. One misstep and you're on the news!

In a 2012 playoff game, the Chicago Bull's Derrick Rose went from being one of the best point guards in the NBA to barely touching the court for two years. While driving to the basket, he took a routine hop and came down awkwardly on his left leg. He has not been the same caliber of athlete since. Not only has he suffered, but so has his team.

Most recently NBA athlete Paul George of the Indiana Pacers was participating in a scrimmage game for Team USA. After trying to block a shot, in a split second, his foot was caught under the base of the basket and he suffered compound fractures of both his tibia and fibula.

A minor misstep could become a big mistake.

Perhaps you feel like you are like my friend April, needing rescue and you are still waiting. Or maybe you feel like Derrick Rose - you made a misstep and years later you are still trying to recover. You may not be able to do much about those steps, but you sure don't want to underestimate the importance of the next one.

For those who walk with God, there is not a single step that is undervalued. Each day is calculated, consulted, and counseled by God. He is there every step of the way. This is what the Psalmist means in Psalm 37:23 when he says that our steps are established by the Lord.

In the Hebrew dictionary the word translated "established" has three primary meanings. "Established" means "to direct or appoint." This means God is *interested* in our steps.

"Established" means "to make ready." This means God is _instructive_ in our steps. The word "established" means "to make firm or to fix." This means God is **involved** in our steps.

Never underestimate the importance of your steps. God doesn't underestimate them. Neither should you. A minor misstep could become a big mistake.

In every step, God is interested. Trust His character.

You make a critical mistake if you believe that God is not interested in the details of your life. You may feel that God is uninterested because you are unimportant. You may not be one of the 40 most influential people under 40 in your city. You may not be a leader in your company. The only picture of you in your high school yearbook is the one they made you take in front of a cheesy background in the cafeteria. You may not think anyone is interested in your steps, but, if you walk with God, He is interested in each one of them. Look at Psalm 37:23 again. If you delight in His way, He will take delight in yours.

Another mistake is to believe that God is interested only in the big things. Whom should I marry? Where should my kids go to school? What should I do with my life? Psalm 37:23 doesn't say God is interested in your leaps. God is interested in your steps. If you will learn to acknowledge God on your way to taking the plunge, you will find that He would not have walked you to the edge of the cliff in the first place. Even big decisions which require great risk are the culmination of many steps.

84

Psalm 37:23 is one of those verses where you will find some variant in the English translations. When you see a verse translated a few different ways from version to version, it doesn't mean that someone is trying to corrupt the Bible. It means there is just no simple way to capture in English what the word in its original language really means. Hebrew is a deep, picturesque language. There may be some words in Hebrew that may be similar, but not quite exact in meaning. There may actually be five or eight English words that come close, but none are an exact match. Those who do the work to translate the Bible into English have to make a choice.

I like the choice of the *New Living Translation*. The NLT says, "*The LORD directs the steps of the godly. He delights in <u>every detail of their lives</u>.*" The qualification for God's involvement is not the size of the step, nor is it the size of the person. For the godly, God is involved in every step.

In theological circles, the involvement of God, not only in our lives, but in the world in general, is referred to as "providence." The word "providence" means "to see before." It is a Biblical doctrine that teaches that God sees what is going to happen before I do. Why? Because not only did He create the world and set it in motion, but He also remains involved. Walking with a providential God who "sees" everything "before" we do changes the way we make decisions.

The fact that our steps are established by the Lord rules out *luck*. Believing that our fate is tied to luck allows us to easily dismiss our choices as having no real bearing on our lives. While it may be true that some things seem to work out better for others, there are a lot of variables in every situation. Information, timing, opportunity, understanding, demand, resources, and skill are all critical considerations for making good decisions. Luck has nothing to do with it.

Another critical factor is whether or not we are godly. According to Psalm 37:23, the question is not whether or not we are lucky, but whether or not we are godly. Godly people will take all of the variables and pray through them. They will make decisions based on what they know pleases the Lord according to Scripture.

People who believe in luck are ultimately lazy and dismissive. They make excuses instead of calculations. If something doesn't work out, it is easier for them to blame it on their lack of luck rather than to evaluate the wisdom of their steps.

Fate is luck on steroids. Fate leads people to believe that no matter what they do, their outcomes are predetermined. The idea of fate brings with it a difficult question, especially in believing in a providential God. How do we know we are not just a puppet on a string?

The scope of this book will not allow me to satisfactorily answer that question for some, but I can offer an idea about providence that will perhaps serve to guide your thoughts on this matter.

"Providence" means not only is God involved in the universe, but He also keeps it consistent. In the middle of the week, because of God's providential care, there may still be "Throw-Back-Thursdays", but there will never be "Walk-on-Water Wednesdays." You will sink on Wednesday in the lake just as quickly as you will sink any other day of the week. It will be that way, your whole life. Because of providence you can teach your children that throwing a rock at someone's head is dangerous and that cotton is soft, without fear that suddenly those truths may be reversed.

God is not deceptive. If He has ordained that certain physical properties of the universe will be as they are and they are as they are, then when He ordains that man make choices that have very real implications on life, then those choices are very real choices. Rocks are rocks and choices are choices. They are real, not fabricated illusions.

Because of the Bible's teaching on providence, it is also a mistake to believe in *deism*. Deism is the idea that God set the world in motion, and then He became uninvolved. Deism was an unbiblical attempt during the Enlightenment to rescue God from evil. During the Enlightenment the world became less superstitious and more scientific. Somehow theologians felt as if they had to rescue a good God from a very scientific, cause-and-effect world that was full of evil. Deism presupposes that evil exists because God is uninvolved in the world.

The relationship between a good God and the existence of evil in the world is referred to in philosophical and theological circles as the question of "theodicy." The issues of theodicy explain why many people profess to be atheists. They can't reconcile the existence of an all-powerful, good God to a very corrupted and evil world. If an all-powerful God who is good exists, then why doesn't He end the world's evil? Logically, then, one of the two must not exist, either an all-powerful, good God doesn't exist or an evil world doesn't exist. Since we can obviously see and experience an evil world, the atheist chooses to exclude an all-powerful, good God from the equation. In atheism, you can't possibly have both.

There is no way to exhaustively answer the questions of theodicy within the scope of this book. Furthermore, there is no capability in my finite mind to do so. But we do know that the Bible teaches that the reality of an evil world does not exclude the involvement of a good God. What the Bible teaches is indeed far more comforting than Deism. God knows the world is evil and He is going to redeem it. I don't want a God who shies away from an evil world. I glory in the fact that we have a powerful and good God who is determined to rescue the world from evil.

As I see it, the flaw with the question of theodicy is that it makes a holistic judgment based on a small sample. It is much like what scientists do with Climate Change, or should we call it the theory formerly known as Global Warming? Scientifically, they can really take only a relatively tiny sample of global temperatures throughout history. Climate-change proponents then make assumptions that the patterns we have seen over the last 70 or so years must be true of climate patterns for thousands of years. There is no consideration that we may be in the midst of a vast cycle of warming and cooling that is consistent with the way God created the world.

In regards to theodicy, the Bible teaches that the world has not always been as it is and it will not always be as it is. The evil we experience currently is only part of a story of redemption that God is bringing to bear for His glory. The Bible gives a very real explanation of why evil is in the world: Man rebelled. The Bible also gives a very real hope to the world: God has sent His Son to seek and to save we who are lost. For us to believe, to any degree, that God is uninvolved in the world contradicts the truth the Psalmist teaches in Psalm 37:23. God has not taken His hands off the steering wheel. He is a good God who establishes the steps of the godly especially in an evil world.

If God is interested and He is good, our response must be to trust His character. Yet, because we live in an evil world with very real threats, there are some instinctive responses that are difficult for us to overcome.

In Psalm 37:1 two of them are mentioned: fret and envy. *"Fret not yourself because of evildoers; be not envious of wrongdoers!"* If a good God is interested in my steps, allowing fear and envy to guide my decisions will lead to major mistakes.

The word "fret" comes from a Hebrew word that means "to kindle a fire." If we are not careful, we will allow certain thoughts and fears to ignite us and guide our decisions. People who walk with a providential God are not driven by fear and fret, but faith.

Economist Steven D. Levitt and writer Stephen J. Dubner teamed up to publish a #1 *New York Times Bestseller* book entitled *Freakonomics.* The book explores the idea of incentive and belief as motivating factors behind the decisions we make. Sometimes the incentives are based on unproven beliefs, which then result in a firestorm of fret and misguided decision making.

If you read their blog, listen to their podcast, and browse their books, you get some interesting insight into the great American freakout. Shoe companies use America's infatuation with exercise and the fear of injury as an incentive to boost sales. Preying upon our unfounded fear, these companies try to persuade consumers that their shoes will help performance and reduce injury. The truth is, despite the fact that our shoes are more advanced than ever, in American athletics we are seeing more knee injuries than ever. In a clever Nike ad, Spike Lee once admired Micheal Jordan and quipped, "It must be the shoes." No, Spike, MJ was a super freak athlete that could have won 6 NBA titles in flip flops. Fret and envy sell shoes, but super-freak athletes win championships.

Truth is, if you run more, there is a natural wear and tear on the body that is unavoidable. Knee injuries have less to do with the shoes and more to do with the nature of running itself. You can invest big money in shoes, but don't underestimate the impact of big mileage on your knees.

In my day if you went to the playground and fell, it was your own fault. Now playgrounds are rubberized and sanitized. You could drop a kid out of a helicopter, and he would bounce on our current-day city park play sets. Why? Because we have convinced parents that playgrounds without rubber are life threatening death traps. A multi-million dollar industry has been birthed from lawsuits that have resulted in civic codes and safety regulations based on a freakout rather than fact.

Case in point of the ultimate parental freakonomic: Do you remember *Baby Einstein*? It was a series of expensive videos produced with colors, shapes, and classical music that took advantage of a time when we believed that if our babies didn't get enough Mozart early on, we had destined them to be dumb. The makers of *Baby Einstein* made millions of dollars based on fear with absolutely no factual proof that their videos increased a child's IQ. But parents bought it because we were conditioned to believe that the way our children turn out is a direct result of the playgrounds we allow them to play on, the shoes we buy for them, and the distance we set them away from the TV while they watch videos of classical music and nursery rhymes. It takes more than a video to educate a child. There is also something in all of us called ability. Just because your kid listens to Mozart before he or she eats solid food doesn't mean he or she will be the next brilliant composer!

Fret and envy can lead to misguided assumptions and major mistakes. People who walk with God should not be so prone to drink the Kool-Aid of America's Freakonomics. Yet, fret is a very real threat.

The Psalmist does something interesting with the word in that he says that you are not to "fret" yourself. It is a reflexive use of the word. In the reflexive sense, "fret" means that you can't control what others do, but you can control how their actions influence you. People are crazy. There is no reason for you to add to their number.

The world will bombard you with information and mistaken assumptions, but it is ultimately your fault if you allow the fire of fret and envy to kindle your thinking.

———————

Envy is also a very real threat to our walk. In the context of Psalm 37, the immediate threat is becoming envious of those who do not know the Lord. When we see godless people do godless things and succeed in a godless system, we should not be surprised. The success of the godless is not a black eye on the record of a providential God.

We go back to the idea of theodicy. The success of the godless is not indicative of the whole story; it is only indicative of the time in which we live. The Psalmist gives the proper perspective on the whole, not just one part. He walks on, understanding that, despite what we may see currently, "*In just a little while, the wicked will be no more; though you look carefully at his place, he will not be there." Psalm 37:10 (ESV)*

Those whose steps are established by the Lord do not make decisions based on the immediate circumstance, but on the distant consequence.

Because God is good and God is interested, we trust His character. Those who walk with God do not make decisions based on the freakout; they make decisions based on who God is. They do not make decisions based on what is happening now, they make decisions based on the big picture of God's providential governance of the world. If we want to go further, we must know where a providential God is going with what He is doing with the world. We want to end up where God is, not where wicked people will forever be. Even though they may enjoy success for only a short while in this life, their ultimate consequence isn't worth it.

The next step needs to be the right step. If we know the God we serve, the times we are in, and the way the world rushes from one freakout to the next, we have no reason to allow that flame of fret and envy to influence our steps. Only a providential God can adequately establish our steps.

To help us refocus and prevent fret and envy from influencing us, the Psalmist gives us some directives that will help us make decisions out of the trust we have in a good, providential God: "Trust in the Lord and do good" (Psalm 37:3a). "Be a friend to faithfulness" (37:3b). To "be a friend of faithfulness" means that you will feed your faith like a shepherd feeds his sheep. Instead of kindling the flames of the freakout, you will feed yourself with information that will establish your steps in faith rather than fear.

The Psalmist goes on: "Delight yourself in the Lord" (37:4). "Commit your way to the Lord" (37:5a). "Trust in Him" (37:5b). "Be still before the Lord and wait patiently for Him" (37:7). "Refrain from anger and forsake wrath" (37:8). "Turn away from evil and do good" (37:27). "Wait for the Lord and keep His way" (37:34). "Mark the blameless and uphold the upright" (37:37).

Our steps are important. The godly walk with a very different posture than we see exhibited in the surrounding culture. As a result, the godly reduce their missteps and their mistakes as they are guided by the trust they have in a good God who is providentially involved in establishing their steps.

In every step, God is instructive. Trust His Word.

Even though we live in a cruel and evil world in which it is easy to take missteps and make mistakes, God's Word remains a sufficient guide, a source of instruction to establish our steps. God's Word prepares us and supports us for life in a world antagonistic to faith.

Trusting God and becoming a student of His Word does not mean that you become aloof to the world. It does not mean that you ignore reality, put on a fake smile, and walk aimlessly, sanctifying stupidity by simply saying, "Whatever happens, I trust

God." If you read Psalm 37, you get a very real sense that the writer understands the difficulty of the culture in which he is living.

The threats are very real. The wicked really do plot against the righteous (37:12a). The idea that they gnash their teeth at him (37:12b) may be somewhat of a metaphor, but there is actual pain involved. In verse 14 the wicked draw the sword and bend their bows to bring down the poor and needy. This phrase describes much of the injustice and tragedy we see going on in the world today.

Trusting God does not exempt us from suffering. From time to time we will be required to walk through some things that we will not enjoy. Even still, God establishes our steps. God's providence is not a sedative that dulls our sense of reality. If anything, God's providence helps bring sobriety to our walk that gives us wisdom to see what is really there.

We said that the word "providence" means "to see before." If this is true, then God's Word helps me see what is ahead. Those who walk with God do not take the world they see at face value. They consult God's Word so that they can see through the situation at hand. Because they are instructed, their steps are not based on where they are now, but on where the step may take them later. *To see through our circumstances, rather than reacting to our circumstances, is critical to going further.* People who trust God's Word are not easily deceived. They look at a situation thoroughly to make sure that a minor misstep does not lead to a tragic mistake.

I am not the adventurer I once was. I have learned that, now that I am older and bigger, I hit the ground harder. When I was in college, I had a friend who enjoyed rock climbing and rappelling. I went with him a few times to a rock ledge on the side of Lookout Mountain in Chattanooga, Tennessee known as *Eagle's Nest*.

In my childhood I was a Boy Scout. Boy Scouts are all about safety. I had been rappelling several times off a tower at summer camp, but that was different. There I had an instructor to constantly check my equipment and a person attached to the rope at the bottom called a belay. At *Eagle's Nest* there is no instructor. There is no belay. Its just you, a rope, rocks, and air between the top and the bottom of the cliff.

My friend and I tied off to a sturdy tree, dropped the rope over the ledge, and attached ourselves to separate lines. Even though I had made a few descents already, something did not feel right about the way I hooked in this particular time. Just before I leaned over the edge and took the first step, something told me I needed to take a minute and look things over. I looked the equipment over several times and could not see a problem. Because of my delay, my friend Jonathan asked me what was going on and he too took a look at my setup.

It has been many years ago, and I can't remember exactly what I had done wrong, but essentially I had threaded the rope through in the wrong direction. Something as small as the direction of the rope would have changed everything.

A minor misstep on the edge of a cliff almost became a huge mistake in my life. God's Word is instructive. You have enough information available in any situation to make the right decision. Don't ignore the details.

Like climbers and rappellers, you need a checklist that will help you not only see to a situation, but also to see through it. You need to be able to discern what is there. I mentioned several of these directives previously, but there are 5 commands in Psalm 37 that become instructive in your steps. To make certain you are not about to make a mistake, ask yourself these questions to be certain you are obeying God's commands. Before you take a step, ask yourself:

- Can I take this step and remain faithful (v. 3)? Will the decision feed faithfulness, or will it lead to my faith becoming weak and anemic?

- Can I take this step with the right attitude (v. 4)? The writer says to "*delight yourself in the Lord, and He will give you the desires of your heart.*" You can't make good decisions based on bad information. I believe you also can't make good decisions with a bad attitude. A lot of us make decisions based on nuisance and annoyance. We avoid people and situations and masquerade it as the call of God on our lives. This is fretting yourself and, as we have discussed, it is a poor basis for decisions, and it will lead to a huge mistake.

The verse says that if you delight in the Lord, He will give you the desires of your heart. I think it is interesting that the note at the beginning of this Psalm tells us that David wrote it. The Bible records an interesting decision David made based on the delight of his heart, in 2 Samuel 7.

David determined that, because the Lord had been so good to him, prospering him and giving him rest from all of his enemies, he would build God a Temple. In consulting the prophet Nathan about the decision, Nathan gives David some interesting advice. *"Go, do all that is in your heart, for the Lord is with you." - 2 Samuel 7:3 (ESV)*

David's attitude in the situation was right. He wanted to do something that honored the Lord. Nathan discerned that David's heart was right. Nathan is essentially saying to David, that he walked so closely to the Lord and was so intent on obeying His Word, what is on his heart is more than likely on God's heart.

Yet, David found out that God did not have the construction of the Temple as the next step. For various reasons, that would be a step God would have David's son take. Yet, God honored David's heart by making a covenant with him that would establish his throne forever.

This passage is instructive to us in affirming that when we delight ourselves in the Lord, He will inform our heart. We have a lot going on in the day. There may not be time to pray and wait days on every decision. If God is providential in every step, how does the walk not become a slow, cumbersome march in which we are paralyzed by every variable and every detail? David learned that, if his delight was in the Lord, he could have confidence in making the next step. If it was not the step God wanted him to take, the Lord would instruct him before he made a mistake.

- Can I take this step and remain committed (v. 5)? The verse says, "*Commit your way to the Lord, trust in Him and He will act.*" As we saw with David's desire to build the Temple, the question is simple: Is it my plan or is it God's plan? The word "commit" here means "to throw your burden to the Lord much like a traveler would throw his pack on a mule." Another way of defining the word is "to roll away."[12] Put the ball in God's court. If He is providential, the burden of the next decision is His, not yours. "*Trust in Him, He will act.*"

- Can I take this step without being rushed (v. 7)? There are two directives in this verse that are counterintuitive to the hurried pace of our life. How can we possibly be productive if we "be still" and "wait patiently"? The contrast in the verse is that of a world in turmoil. It is the godless going nuts.

Two of the favorite words in our culture seem to be *rush* and *push*. Everything is pushed on us. In an image driven, media saturated culture of instant information we are rushed and pushed instead of being allowed to process and make the proper decision. My friend Renny Scott has a wise saying pertinent for the point. He says, "Satan pushes, God leads."

In the midst of the chaos is a calm that characterizes those who trust a good, providential God at His Word. As we saw in the chapter on Pace, there is more to the Christian walk than miracles. The Christian walk is more about what God teaches us in the waiting.

- Can I take the next step with pure, unselfish motives (v. 8)? What is true of attitude also holds true for motive. We can't make good decisions with a bad attitude. This verse takes it a step further. It is impossible to take the right step for the wrong reason. Anger, wrath, and fret, according to the Psalm, "*tend only to evil.*" Apple seeds do not produce orange trees, and sinful motives will not yield righteous results.

The early spring seems to bring with it an infestation of wasps inquiring about nesting at my house. We have a covered, screened-in back porch. Due to the way it is built, it is easy for wasps to come up through the floor and then remain trapped inside the screen. Apparently wasps have short memories. They are good at entrance but poor at escape.

Along with our family of rocking chairs sits a can of wasp spray. We usually place the can on a ledge that is attached to the screen. There are times that the can, the screen, and a fatally trapped wasp make for the most ironic scene. So many times the wasps crawl up the screen beside a can that contains for them 20 ounces of instant death. Minor misstep. Big mistake. Why? Because not only do wasps have short memories, they can't read.

When we fail to spend time in God's Word and be instructed by it, we are prone to take steps into dangerous places. We take what we think to be minor steps and make huge mistakes. God has given us the right information so that we can make the right decisions in a dangerous world. If you want to go far, read the Book!

In every step, God is involved. Trust His power.

"Providence" means that God is not only interested in what we do and instructive about what we do, but He has His hand on what we do.

Throughout Psalm 37 is the theme of "land." The idea of "land" basically comes down to this: This is God's world, we are just paying rent. Right now there are godly and ungodly people living on God's land. Everyone gets an opportunity. God is keeping record of what we do with our opportunity.

Currently it seems as if the wicked prosper, but suddenly a day will come when everything changes. In His providence, God takes what is wrong and makes it right. There is a sense of reversal throughout the passage. In verse 14 the wicked draw the sword and the bow against the poor and needy. In verse 15 the swords of the wicked enter their own hearts. In verse 10 the wicked have a place and they may even seem to prosper in it. Yet, by the end of the verse they are no longer there. When God brings His righteous judgment, the wicked will not survive. *"For they will soon fade like grass and wither like the green herb."* - *Psalm 37:2 (ESV)*

The Lord is powerful. At some point the opportunity that the wicked have to repent in the land will draw to a close. You may even be someone who does not think it is important to have your steps established by the Lord. You feel you are doing well as you are. Everything you touch prospers and comes up green. That may be true, but please remember, *summer doesn't last forever* (37:2).

For the godly who walk with the Lord, the threat of God's judgment is ominous, but the godly are comforted because they will be saved in judgment rather than destroyed by it. *"For the arms of the wicked shall be broken, but the LORD upholds the righteous."* - Psalm 37:17 (ESV)

In fact, the situation for the godly will change just as drastically as it does for the ungodly in the judgment. The godly who live like strangers in the land suddenly inherit it (37:9, 11). The Lord is powerful and involved. He knows those who are His and He will, in His providence, establish their steps so that they will eventually inherit the land.

The hope that God's providential involvement brings applies not only to the future. We are also beneficiaries in the present. In verses 23-25, David says, *"The steps of a man are established by the LORD, when he delights in his way; though he fall, he shall not be cast headlong, for the LORD upholds his hand. I have been young, and now am old, yet I have not seen the righteous forsaken or his children begging for bread."*

While reflecting on an experience in battle, David praises the Lord: *"You gave a wide place for my steps under me, and my feet did not slip."* 2 Samuel 22:37 (ESV) In the chaos of the battlefield, the Lord was powerfully involved in the details of David's walk as a warrior. Even the placement of David's feet in the fight was a detail God did not overlook.

Psalm 18:1 and 2 reads, *"I love you, O LORD, my strength, The LORD is my rock and my fortress and my deliverer, my God, my rock, in whom I take refuge, my shield, and the horn of my salvation, my stronghold."*

According to the prescript on this Psalm, David penned it on a day when he experienced rescue from his enemies, particularly Saul. No doubt, in the heat of the moment, for those who trust the Lord, the application of God acting as our strength and our refuge becomes apparent. Our walk with Him deepens in the experience of the trial. Yet, I wonder how often God acts as "my shield" and I walk away unaware?

The father of our student pastor's wife holds a critically important position. Her father Micah, is the director of the Homeland Security Division for the Georgia Emergency Management Agency/Homeland Security (GEMA/HS). He probably has a faceplate on his desk that weighs 12 pounds! I'm sure when you ask Micah, "How was your day?" there is only a certain percentage of that answer that you really want to know. For the percentage left unanswered, fill your imagination with *The Blacklist*, *NCIS*, *24*, and a smattering of other crime shows in which we are exposed to the terrorist underworld for 60 minutes with commercial interruption. The difference in our day and Micah's day is that we can safely turn off the television and it all goes away. He can't.

When something blows up, you'll know about Micah's office. But I wonder how many things haven't blown up and you had no idea Micah was there!

There is so much going on in the world that I don't want to know. I like to sleep. While I sleep peacefully, I wonder how great is God's grace as our shield? How often does He protect me, and I am unaware? Psalm 18:2 reminds me that He is there when I need Him as my shield, my rock, my strength, my fortress, and my deliverer. Psalm 18:2 reminds me that He is there even when I am unaware of how desperately I need Him. How many things in my life were so close to blowing up, and I walked away from my shield ungrateful and unaware that He was there?

Because God is powerfully involved, He is able not only to protect, but to change even the most dire of situations. Knowing this motivates our prayer life. We do not trust luck. We do not chalk it up to fate. We do not believe in the false idealogical idol of Deism. We pray to a very real God who has His hand on every situation. Listen to what David says in Psalm 40:1-4:

> "I waited patiently for the LORD;
>> he inclined to me and heard my cry.
> He drew me up from the pit of destruction,

out of the miry bog,
and set my feet upon a rock,
making *my steps* secure.
He put a new song in my mouth,
a song of praise to our God.
Many will see and fear,
and put their trust in the LORD.
Blessed is the man who makes
the LORD his trust,
who does not turn to the proud,
to those who go astray after a lie!"

The phrase used in Psalm 37:11 that "the meek shall inherit the land" was quoted by Jesus in Matthew 5:5. Ultimately, the interest, instruction, and involvement we find in God's providence is fulfilled in God's Son. All that the Lord has determined to do will be accomplished by Jesus. Currently, He is gathering a people whose steps are established by the Lord and who will inherit the land. They are able to navigate a difficult world as it is now because they serve a God who is interested. They take steps that are instructed. They are helped by the hand of a mighty God who is always involved. Though one may stumble along the way "*he shall not be cast headlong, for the LORD upholds his hand*" - Psalm 37:24 (ESV) **Even his missteps are not ultimate mistakes.**

Why? The steps of those who desire to go further are established by the Lord. Those who walk with Him have a good God who is providentially interested. The godly trust His character. We have a good God who is providentially instructive. The godly trust His Word. We have a good God who is providentially involved. The godly trust His power.

Provision

For the LORD God is a sun and shield; the LORD bestows favor and honor. No good thing does he withhold from those who walk uprightly. O LORD of hosts, blessed is the one who trusts in you!
- Psalm 84:11-12 (ESV)

When I was younger, I did a fair amount of hiking and camping. The destination determined what we took. If we were going to camp for several days in one place, what we packed looked very different than what we would take if we were going to hike overnight. The season also had a lot to say about how we packed. Warm nights called for different clothing and equipment than cold ones.

One of the most interesting places I have visited is the Mountain Crossings Store at Neel's Gap in Blairsville, Georgia. Construction of the store was completed in 1937, the same year as the completion of the Appalachian Trail. The store actually sits on the trail and represents the only covered portion of the 2,100 mile journey.[13]

Someone walking from Georgia to Maine on the Appalachian Trail is referred to as a *thru-hiker*. *Thru-hikers* get to the Mountain Crossings Store on the third day of their hike after their first major ascent and descent of the highest point in Georgia, fittingly known as "Blood Mountain."

Walking along the trail, your eyes are drawn to the most unique sight as you approach the Mountain Crossings Store. Covering the walkway is a massive tree full of shoes hanging from its branches. And I don't mean just a few shoes, I'm talking hundreds of them.

The reason for the shoe tree is that three days into the journey, most of the *thru-hikers* realize they are ill prepared for the trail ahead. Boots that may look serious in a sporting goods store are no match for the AT. Feeling defeated, the hikers enter the store, approach the counter, and that is where the real work begins.

The staff at the store evaluates more than 500 packs a year and ships home over 9,000 pounds of stuff the hikers thought they needed. The shoes in the tree are a testimony to the fact that if you are going to be successful on a thru-hike, you've got to get rid of what you don't need. If you are going to go a long way, you can't be unnecessarily weighted down with stuff.

The experience of the store is fittingly described by one of the hikers who blogged about his journey as the place "where the outfitter's staff patiently explains to physically busted, emotionally blasted thru-hikers how much happier they'll be when they mail all their unnecessary crap home."[14]

The Bible pictures those who walk with God as *thru-hikers*. *"Beloved, I urge you as **sojourners** and exiles to abstain from the* *passions of the flesh, which wage war against your soul.*" - 1 Peter 2:11 (ESV)

We are the hikers and God is the packer. "*As for the rich in this present age, charge them not to be haughty, nor to set their hopes on the uncertainty of riches, but on **God, who richly provides us with everything to enjoy.**" - 1 Timothy 6:17 (ESV)*

The Bible plainly teaches that all things come from God. For those who walk with God, this truth helps to keep a proper perspective on their stuff. When David took an offering sufficient enough to build the Temple, he offered this perspective in a thanksgiving prayer to God.

"*But who am I, and what is my people, that we should be able thus to offer willingly? **For all things come from you, and of your own have we given you. For we are strangers before you and sojourners, as all our fathers were.** Our days on the earth are like a shadow, and there is no abiding. O LORD our God, all this abundance that we have provided for building you a house for your holy name comes from your hand and is all your own.*" - 1 Chronicles 29:14-16 (ESV)

Even though the people gave the offering, David realized what was really happening. The stuff that God had given to them they were giving back to Him. The stuff they had acquired for the conquering of the Promised Land would be repacked for the next leg of the journey - construction of the Temple.

If you and I are thru-hikers and God is the packer: take inventory of your life and you will realize that there is a ***story in*** pen up your pack and look. What God has given you may have been necessary for the journey thus far, but it may be useless, perhaps even a hindrance, for the next leg of your life. If you look at your stuff with the right perspective, you may be able to see your next step. If you want to go further, you must be willing to walk up to the counter and allow the packer to rid your life of unnecessary stuff.

With this chapter I want to summarize a survey of Biblical truths into four principles that will help you see the story of your stuff.

Principle #1 - God is a joyous and generous giver.

The Bible says in Psalm 84:11-12, *"For the LORD God is a sun and shield; the LORD bestows favor and honor. No good thing does he withhold from those who walk uprightly. O LORD of hosts, blessed is the one who trusts in you!"*

God has created a world in which there is adequate supply for every person to experience both provision (daily needs) and abundance (bountiful blessing).[15] Even in leading Israel out of Egypt as a slave nation, He did not leave them empty-handed for the journey to the promised land. Yet, He also did not give them everything they needed to successfully complete the journey. Along the way He created for them an experience. It was a story in their stuff.

Along the way He packed and repacked their provisions to teach them a truth necessary for going further. God was not only their deliverer, He was also their provider. In Deuteronomy

8:2-10, Moses stands before a new generation and rehearses the story in their stuff, the experiences God created for them to teach them to depend on Him as their provider.

"*And you shall remember the whole way that the LORD your God has led you these forty years in the wilderness, that he might humble you, testing you to know what was in your heart, whether you would keep his commandments or not. And he humbled you and let you hunger and fed you with manna, which you did not know, nor did your fathers know, that he might make you know that man does not live by bread alone, but man lives by every word that comes from the mouth of the LORD. Your clothing did not wear out on you and your foot did not swell these forty years. Know then in your heart that, as a man disciplines his son, the LORD your God disciplines you. So you shall keep the commandments of the LORD your God by walking in his ways and by fearing him. For the LORD your God is bringing you into a good land, a land of brooks of water, of fountains and springs, flowing out in the valleys and hills, a land of wheat and barley, of vines and fig trees and pomegranates, a land of olive trees and honey, a land in which you will eat bread without scarcity, in which you will lack nothing, a land whose stones are iron, and out of whose hills you can dig copper. And you shall eat and be full, and you shall bless the LORD your God for the good land he has given you.*" - *Deuteronomy 8:2-10 (ESV)*

In the story of stuff, there are moments of abundance, times of bountiful blessing in which you receive far more than you need or deserve. In the story of stuff there are also moments of provision. These may be crisis moments in which you realize you barely have enough. In provision, there may be no crisis at all. It is simply that you have what you need, move on. At each stage of our journey the stuff we have tells a story. It is a story of how we go here. It is also a story of what the next step may be.

Notice that Moses actually said that God humbled them and allowed them to hunger, then fed them manna so they would learn that *"man does not live by bread alone, but man lives by every word that comes from the mouth of the LORD."* If you are to successfully complete the thru-hike that God has planned for you, it may be expedient to look at your stuff and discern God's hand in abundance and provision; the lessons of dependence.

Maybe you have so much stuff you are deceived by the illusion of self-sufficiency. Notice what the Lord said in Deuteronomy 8: Even the land in all of its blessing is a provision of abundance from God. To go far, even in our abundance, we need to foster a perspective of blessing and dependence. We have what we have because God has given it to us.

Principle # 2 - Sin has distorted the story of stuff.

We stated that God created a world in which there would be enough resources for everyone to experience provision and abundance. Yet, there is a contradiction in our theology and our experience at this point. If there is plenty of stuff, why doesn't everyone have enough?

In the garden narrative (Gen. 1-3), the Bible teaches that sin would not only bring physical death to humanity, but it would cause havoc in every system of life. Sin would bring about not only a physical curse, but also an ecological one. We would inherit not only a decaying world from Adam, but one that was also grossly distorted.

Even the economy of the planet would be impacted. Man would eat bread only by the sweat of his face. He would work diligently in a world that was designed to work with him, but now it would return only thorns and thistles. These words are not merely ecological, they are also economic.

And to Adam he said, "Because you have listened to the voice of your wife and have eaten of the tree of which I commanded you, 'You shall not eat of it,' cursed is the ground because of you; in pain you shall eat of it all the days of your life; thorns and thistles it shall bring forth for you; and you shall eat the plants of the field. By the sweat of your face you shall eat bread, till you return to the ground, for out of it you were taken; for you are dust, and to dust you shall return." - Genesis 3:17-19 (ESV)

There are three reasons why people may not have enough in a sin cursed world: *disruption, destruction,* and *disaster*.

Disruption

Disruption is the interruption of systems of delivery, whether it be education, food supply, safety, or health care. The *Theology of Work Project*, a group of Christian writers exploring all that the Bible says about work and the work-place, reports on their website that about 1.4 billion people in the world lack the basic necessities of life.[16] Even in America there are many who live hand-to-mouth. Globally, over a billion people live hand-to-mouth. Much of it is caused by disruption.

Some economic channels of delivery are disrupted due to war. For example, in Africa or South America we see violent drug cartels or tribal militias that disrupt supplies of food and other forms of aid.

In other contexts, selfishness becomes a great source of disruption. Whether through very low wages or by the blatant reaping of resources, adequate provision for one group of people is funneled toward more wealthy people to satisfy their appetites.

There are plenty of cities and rural areas in our nation where a child is born having much less of an opportunity of quality education and health care as a child born in another community. Whatever the cause, each of these places has a story in its stuff. There is a reason for the disruption that needs to be identified and rectified. God is a joyous and generous giver. Disrupted people are not experiencing His abundance and provision. More importantly, these people are disrupted not only in receiving provision, but they are probably disrupted also from hearing the preaching of the gospel.

Destruction

In other contexts, God's provision and abundance may not be interrupted; they may have adequate channels of economic delivery, but they are being wasted and destroyed. Destruction has a myriad of causes, including addiction, violence, poor work habits, poor choices with resources and finances, or bad environmental management.

Destroyed areas that may be otherwise fertile are contaminated or mismanaged in such a way that provision is no longer available. We were living in Birmingham, Alabama in 2010 when the Deepwater Horizon oil rig exploded in the Gulf of Mexico. Our state's economy was already suffering, not only because of the economic downturn, but, like other Gulf Coast states, we were still recovering somewhat from the blow caused by Hurricane Katrina in 2005.

Depending heavily on tourism to stimulate the economy, the gulf coast area was just beginning to have profitable seasons again when the oil spill destroyed the coast line. It was the end not only of a tourist season, but it also caused contamination of a vital food supply and disrupted the harvesting of many of our state's natural resources in the Gulf of Mexico. The trickle-down effect of the oil spill impacted every person in our state, no matter how close or how distant from the coast one lived.

Other people live in communities of bountiful supply, but they destroy the provision delivered to them by making poor choices. There are a lot of children who suffer greatly either because their parents do not choose to work or perhaps because they waste what little they do have on the purchase of drugs, gambling, or buying frivolous things that are not needful. For some, debt is as destructive as drug addiction.

If you look at your provision and you do not see enough, ask yourself a difficult question: Would there be plenty, perhaps even abundance, if you made better choices with the resources and abilities you have? You will not go far if you continue to destroy your stuff.

Disaster

We live in a world that is in environmental turmoil. Environmentalists point to "man-made" climate change. This may be a microscopic part of the whole. The meta-narrative of Scripture does not point to "man-made" climate change, but rather to "sin-induced" climate change. Our biggest problem with the climate is not coming out of the tail pipe of our cars or an aerosol can, but rather it is evidence of the curse.

We live in a world of catastrophic storms, tornados, hurricanes, heat waves, floods, drought, and disease. The prices of our food market are vulnerable and prone to swing wildly when there is some sort of disaster that impacts the harvest. God's people need to be mindful and compassionate toward those who have suffered disaster. A context of provision and abundance may suddenly find itself not only economically lacking, but emotionally devastated.

Whatever the cause - disruption, destruction, or disaster - there are many who look in their packs and see a distorted story in their stuff. What should be there, isn't. It is hard to go far when you don't have what you need.

Principle #3 - *We are called to be stewards, not consumers.*

What is the difference between a steward and a consumer? The difference is in the way one views his stuff. Stewards manage things. Their attitude is *contentment*. The by-product of the steward is *more*.

Stewards maintain. They make sure some resources stay productive, useable, and workable.

Stewards multiply. They make wise investments and take what they have and turn it into more.

Stewards distribute. Stewards become a conduit of delivery to others. They are wise in trade.

Stewards produce. Stewards are able to combine resources and make them more valuable by creating something that is in demand.

Stewards protect. They see the value of what they have and also see the value in what others have. They are wise, not wasteful.

Paul had a great relationship of stewardship with the church in Phillipi. Recorded in Scriptures is Paul's report to his supporters concerning the status of his mission. This conversation exemplifies perfectly the attitude and principles of stewardship. Notice the indications of maintenance, multiplication, distribution, production, and protection that are within these paragraphs:

I rejoiced in the Lord greatly that now at length you have revived your concern for me. You were indeed concerned for me, but you had no opportunity. Not that I am speaking of being in need, for I have learned in whatever situation I am to be content. I know how to be brought low, and I know how to abound (maintenance). In any and every circumstance, I have learned the secret of facing plenty and hunger, abundance and need. I can do all things through him who strengthens me. Yet it was kind of you to share my trouble (distribution). And you Philippians yourselves know that in the beginning of the gospel, when I left Macedonia, no church entered into partnership with me in giving and receiving, except you only. Even in Thessalonica you sent me help for my needs once and again. Not that I seek the gift, but I seek the fruit that increases to your credit. I have received full payment, and more. I am well supplied, having received from Epaphroditus the gifts you sent (production), a fragrant offering, a sacrifice acceptable and pleasing to God. And my God will supply every need of yours according to his riches in glory in Christ Jesus (protection). To our God and Father be glory forever and ever. Amen. - Philippians 4:10-20 (ESV)

Stewards manage things. Consumers use things up. The consumer attitude is *greed*. The by-product is *waste*. In the desperate pursuit to consume more and more the consumer ends up with less and less. With no thought of faithfulness toward God in the elements of management and stewardship, the consumer eventually finds himself in a desert land. In Jeremiah 17:5-11, the prophet of God warns the people of the end result of consumerism:[17]

Thus says the Lord: 'Cursed is the man who trusts in man and makes flesh his strength, whose heart turns away from the LORD. He is like a shrub in the desert, and shall not see any good come. He shall dwell in the parched places of the wilderness, in an uninhabited salt land. "Blessed is the man who trusts in the LORD, whose trust is the LORD. He is like a tree planted by water, that sends out its roots by the stream, and does not fear when heat comes, for its leaves remain green, and is not anxious in the year of drought, for it does not cease to bear fruit.' The heart is deceitful above all things, and desperately sick; who can understand it? 'I the LORD search the heart and test the mind, to give every man according to his ways, according to the fruit of his deeds.' Like the partridge that gathers a brood that she did not hatch, so is he who gets riches but not by justice; in the midst of his days they will leave him, and at his end he will be a fool.

A lesson quickly learned in hiking is that consuming resources instead of managing them is not wise. On an overnight backpacking trip, I once packed everything I loved to eat. There was a maximum weight limit for my pack, and I was determined to fill it to the brim with my favorite things.

Starting up the trail, I began to consume. It was not long before I was sluggish, sick, and sorely lacking what I really needed to complete the trail. Even worse, I was destined to carry a pack that was heavily weighed down with wasted stuff I didn't need.

Successful thru-hikers know how to be stewards of their stuff. A proper management plan is essential if you want to go far.

Principle #4 - The Gospel gives us a redemptive lens through which we can inventory our stuff and take the next step.

The death, burial, and resurrection of Jesus Christ is not simply a plan that shows people how to go to Heaven; it is a demonstration of Lordship. When Jesus rose from the dead, He was certainly Savior, but He was also confirmed as Lord of all. If you have asked for Christ's forgiveness of sin, but have no intention of submitting to Him as Lord, you do not adequately understand the Gospel message. We come to Him for salvation, not only for what He has done, but because of who He is. Salvation means that not only have we been rescued, but it also demands that we be submitted. Jesus asks a piercing question: *"Why do you call me 'Lord, Lord,' and not do what I tell you?"* - *Luke 6:46 (ESV)*

Allow me to invite you to do something spiritually that I saw powerfully demonstrated at the Mountain Crossings Store. Bring everything in your pack to the counter. Let the expert take out what you don't need, add what you do need, and repack it in a way that it will be more manageable for the next step. Remember, walking with God describes the way we do everything, not some things. Biblically, there is no separation between our spiritual life and our material one. The story of your stuff is a part of your walk. Bring everything to the table and submit it to God for repacking.

As you do so, ask three questions:

Question #1 - Am I stranded?

You may look at the story of your stuff and realize, "I'm stuck!" You are at a place in the trail where you can't move forward, and there is no going back. There may be several reasons. Perhaps you are a victim of disruption, destruction, or disaster. Perhaps you have been more of a consumer instead of a steward and have destroyed your resources. For whatever reason, you have had a change of heart and you are ready to walk with God.

If you are stranded, pray for God's help, seek guidance in God's Word, and seek community in God's people. Several passages of Scripture invite us to ask what we need from the Lord (Matthew 7:7-11, John 14:13, 1 John 5:14). James 4:1-3 instructs us not only to ask, but to be careful that we do not do so with an attitude of consumerism, which, in community, causes chaos. *"What causes quarrels and what causes fights among you? Is it not this, that your passions are at war within you? You desire and do not have, so you murder. You covet and cannot obtain, so you fight and quarrel. You do not have, because you do not ask. You ask and do not receive, because you ask wrongly, to spend it on your passions."*

Whether you need resources to continue in school, start a new job, or open a new business, asking is not out of the question. Perhaps you lack a skill or an ability. It is amazing the collection of people God has gathered in the church community. The church is not only a resource for faith, but for those who are invested and connected, the church becomes a valuable help for those who are stranded.

Question #2 - Am I stagnant?

If you are stagnant, lighten the load. You have found that, like many of the hikers approaching the Mountain Crossings Store, you are busted and bruised. You have too much, and what you do have is not adequate for the journey ahead. It sounds strange to say, but it is often true. When we go from provision to abundance, we may grow fat and ungrateful if we are not careful. Over time, we lose perspective and actually think we need more than we actually do. Instead of being generous distributors, we become ungrateful hoarders. Moses warned God's people of this in Deuteronomy 8:11-20:

Take care lest you forget the LORD your God by not keeping his commandments and his rules and his statutes, which I command you today, lest, when you have eaten and are full and have built good houses and live in them, and when your herds and flocks multiply and your silver and gold is multiplied and all that you have is multiplied, then your heart be lifted up, and you forget the LORD your God, who brought you out of the land of Egypt, out of the house of slavery, who led you through the great and terrifying wilderness, with its fiery serpents and scorpions and thirsty ground where there was no water, who brought you water out of the flinty rock, who fed you in the wilderness with manna that your fathers did not know, that he might humble you and test you, to do you good in the end. Beware lest you say in your heart, "My power and the might of my hand have gotten me this wealth." You shall remember the LORD your God, for it is he who gives you power to get wealth, that he may confirm his covenant that he swore to your fathers, as it is this day. And if you forget the LORD your God and go after other gods and serve them and worship them, I solemnly warn you today that you shall surely perish. Like the nations that the LORD makes to perish before you, so shall you perish, because you would not obey the voice of the LORD your God.

We need to keep the humble perspective that God is our provider. Ask these important questions:

- *Do I have things that are wasting my resources?* It may be a hobby or a home that is too expensive for you to maintain. It is draining your resources and, in so doing, drying up your chance to take the steps God desires for you to take.

- *Do I have things that are wasting my time?* Time is as valuable as money. You may not be able to financially afford to give or do certain things. The next step may not require your money, but your time. Investing too much time in things that ultimately don't matter is just as much of a drain of an important resource as financial debt. Some people are in a financial place of stagnation; others are at the same place because of the way they use their time. Perhaps better time management or more efficiency during times of work will help you here. Learn to say "no" and recover your valuable resource of time.

• *Do I have things in my life that are draining me physically?* Sleep and nutrition are as essential to your walk with God as your time and money. Some people can't take the next step because they are so tired. Do you work too much? Your insatiable appetite to get the job done may actually be causing you to become less productive. Video games are fun, but playing them all night will actually turn you into a zombie. You are not moving to the next step because you are not sleeping. You may not be able to do everything the recreation league wants you to do if you are going to do what God wants you to do. Your strength and health are a valuable resource in the walk.

• *Do I have things in my life that are taking a toll on my family emotionally?* I love sports, but we are at a point in which I think we have lost our way. As a pastor and a parent, my observation about the current state of year-round, everyday practice, travel-team sports is that it is not good for family dynamics. Most of the time, I find that it is not good for the marriage and what most people refuse to acknowledge is that their kids don't even enjoy it. The ultimate goal is a college scholarship. Yet, once the scholarship is in hand, the student athlete is sick of the sport and fails to complete his commitment to the school. Back home are two parents who still live together but don't really know each other anymore. For years their attention has been on sports instead of on going further in their marriage. It may not be travel teams for you, but there may be other things desperately out of balance that are preventing you and your family from taking the next step.

• *Are there things in my life keeping me out of God's will spiritually?* There may be things in your life that God doesn't want you to have and He doesn't want you to do. Instead of feeding faith, as we discussed in a previous chapter, they are strangling your faith. You are in God's Word less and less and you are AWOL on the people of God. It is hard to take the next step in your walk with God when you are holding on or holding out on things out of the will of God. God doesn't bless disobedience, He punishes it.

Question #3 - *What can I share?*

Acts 2:44-45 is a powerful example of a sharing faith community. Their sharing was an essential element in their witness of the gospel to the culture around them. There may be things in your pack that were useful to you in getting you where you are, but they are useless to you in the days ahead. If you would allow God to place those things in someone else's pack, those things may help them go further. You may not be able to take it as far as they can. Let them have it for the glory of God!

One of the unique things that happens on the Appalachian Trail is that it becomes a resourceful community of sharing. I have heard numerous stories of packs of thru-hikers helping one another take the next step as they literally pass things back and forth along the trail. In a place where provision is otherwise scarce, because of the hiker's attitude of stewardship and willingness to distribute, there is plenty.

There may be people you know whose packs have been devastated by disruption, destruction, or disaster. You may be an incredible blessing to them, and it may help you move forward if you will take the abundance in your pack and allow it to become provision in their pack.

If you want to go further in any venue of life, look at the story of your stuff. Before you are busted and bruised by the next step, walk up to the counter and submit it to the packer. Watch His work as He removes, rearranges, restores, replenishes, and readies your pack for the next step of the journey. Remember, He knows what's next and He knows what you need to go further.

Priority

Finally, then, brothers, we ask and urge you in the Lord Jesus, that as you received from us how you ought to walk and to please God, just as you are doing, that you do so more and more.
- 1 Thessalonians 4:1 (ESV)

Throughout the book I continue to mention that walking with God does not describe the way you do some things; it describes the way you do everything. Walking with God is life-altering and all consuming.

To declare that the walk is all-consuming is a lot to say to a person who has a lot going on. Life demands attention. I am sure, like everyone else, you are an extremely busy person. But do you realize that according to Scripture, God has ultimately called you to only one thing? *The one thing God requires of you is to walk in a way that pleases Him.* Paul says in 1 Thessalonians 4:1 that you and I "ought to walk and please God."

Honestly, I'm not a big fan of the circus. Even though there is a lot going on in the three rings, something about the chaos of it just doesn't hold my attention. Trapeze doesn't do it for me. If you are a circus clown and you are reading this book, I'm sorry to offend you, but what you do in the circus doesn't connect with me. However, I would love to know how so many of you get in those little cars. Other than that, I'm not a fan of the clown. The dog trainer part of the show is absolute torture for me. They are about to fire a man out of a canon. Do the circus people seriously believe that a poodle hopping through a hoop is supposed to psyche me up for the human cannonball? Get the little dogs off the floor and let's see a guy fly through the air like a missile. I see dogs everyday. Missile men - not so much.

There is one point of the circus, however, that grips me. Bring out the lions and the tigers, and I'm all in. Those massive majestic animals are mesmerizing. Put a guy in there with the real potential of being mauled right before my eyes - I'm all over that - from a safe spectator distance, of course!

Have you ever noticed that the lion tamer takes only two things into the cage with him? He takes a whip, which I can understand, and a chair, which I cannot. Yet in that infamous image of the lion tamer that is etched in our minds, you see only two things in his hands, a whip and a chair.

Most of the time when we watch the lion tamer work his craft, we are excited by the whip, but think little of the chair. But the chair is the most important element of all. The whip has little to do with influencing the animals.

With the whip, the lion tamer controls the crowd. We love the crack of the whip and, as humans, we are sympathetic to the sting. Indiana Jones may do it for humans, but Indy does nothing for lions. The whip may capture our attention, but it is with the chair that the lion tamer controls the beast.

Lions have an impeccable ability to focus. When the end of the chair is extended toward a lion, the lion becomes almost paralyzed. Now, instead of focusing on one thing, the leg end of the chair presents the beast with four. The otherwise perfectly focused animal doesn't know what to do next. He has too many choices to make.

A powerful creature out of focus is ineffective.

I find myself like the lion a lot of times. I have so much in front of me that I lose focus and become ineffective. I find myself looking at the leg end of the chair way too much.

In a lot of ways, it is easy to become confused and paralyzed in your walk, wondering what to do next. You have too many things in front of you at one time. This is why priority is so important. When it comes to your walk, *the first thing determines everything*. With so many things in our vision, how does one possibly narrow it all down to one thing? The good news is that God has made it an easy choice for you. *Remember, God has ultimately called you to do only one thing, walk in a way that pleases Him.*

Jesus said it like this, *"Therefore do not be anxious, saying, 'What shall we eat?' or 'What shall we drink?' or 'What shall we wear?' For the Gentiles seek after all these things, and your heavenly Father knows that you need them all. But seek first the kingdom of God and his righteousness, and all these things will be added to you." - Matthew 6:31-33 (ESV)*

What we eat, drink, or wear is the leg end of the chair. Jesus teaches us that if we can get those things in the right order of priority and make the *one* thing the *main* thing, all of those other things God will provide. Remember, He is the provider for those who walk with Him.

That word *seek*, Jesus uses in the passage, means "to walk with focus." It describes investigation and searching. You can't seek several things. There is an old proverb that says, "He who chases two rabbits captures none." The only way you can truly seek something is to get it down to one.

If you could get four or five things out of your face and bring one thing into focus, it would help you go further. Why, because according to Jesus in Matthew 6:31-33, **the first thing determines everything**. Allow me to pull several Scriptures together and expound the idea.

If the first thing is the wrong thing, everything else will suffer.

Wonderful things become horrible gods. The ancients would make for themselves a wide range of idols representing the various gods. The essential hope was that each idol would bring protection and prosperity in some area of life. The end result was not prosperity, but foolishness.

God brought a message on the idiocy of their idolatry through the prophet Isaiah. He said,

"All who fashion idols are nothing, and the things they delight in do not profit. Their witnesses neither see nor know, that they may

be put to shame. Who fashions a god or casts an idol that is profitable for nothing? Behold, all his companions shall be put to shame, and the craftsmen are only human. Let them all assemble, let them stand forth. They shall be terrified; they shall be put to shame together." - Isaiah 44:9-11 (ESV)

In the prophet's perspective, the people put great priority on something that was essentially nothing; a lifeless, powerless, empty nothing. The prophet goes on to say about their idols,

"They know not, nor do they discern, for he has shut their eyes, so that they cannot see, and their hearts, so that they cannot understand. No one considers, nor is there knowledge or discernment to say, 'Half of it I burned in the fire; I also baked bread on its coals; I roasted meat and have eaten. And shall I make the rest of it an abomination? Shall I fall down before a block of wood?' He feeds on ashes; a deluded heart has led him astray, and he cannot deliver himself or say, 'Is there not a lie in my right hand?'" - Isaiah 44:18-20 (ESV)

In the end, the people were so drunk on their idols that they could not see the foolishness of their bowing down to a block of wood that they had carved themselves. The idols were unresponsive and inadequate to meet the people's deepest needs. In their desperate search for prosperity, they failed to realize that the idols they had created were unable to ultimately deliver. The final words of the passage are most piercing. The people were so blinded by idolatry that they could not see that it was all a lie in their right hand.

Football is an incredible game, but it is a horrible god. Work is a noble activity, but it is a horrible god. Youth league sports can be a fun thing, but it is a horrible god. Money is a necessary thing, but it is a horrible god. We fail to see that many of the things we prop up as our main priority, in the hopes that they will bring us happiness and prosperity, are lies in our right hand. We are fools bowing to a block of wood.

Parasites find life only by sucking the life out of their host. The word "seek" Jesus uses in Matthew 6:31-33 means not only to investigate, but it also means "to seek the life of." It means to grab the essence, to get something out of it that adds life to you.

So many times we move wonderful things into the place of priority thinking they will add to our life. In the end, we find instead that they are parasites.

If you put a parasite as the priority of your life everyone else around you will suffer. The time you should be loving and teaching your children, you are farming out to a trainer or a coach to develop their skills for a game. The attention you should be giving your spouse is spent in a hobby that has become a priority. As such it is a parasite to your marriage. In certain seasons of your child's development, in certain seasons of your marriage, a parasite will destroy the essential nutrients of the attention and devotion you should be giving to those seasons of life. Your children are seeking life from you, but instead, you may be handing them over to things that are sucking the life out of them.

When it comes time for your children to bear fruit, you will find that, because of the parasites, there is nothing there. The kids are athletic, but empty. There is money, but no marriage. Your golf score is great, but the influence you should have in your home is gone. You don't need a longer list of examples. You can identify the parasites in your priorities much better than I.

If the first thing is a wellspring, everything else finds new life.

In a conversation Jesus was having with a woman at a well, He said, *"Everyone who drinks of this water will be thirsty again, but whoever drinks of the water that I will give him will never be thirsty again. The water that I will give him will become in him a spring of water welling up to eternal life." - John 4:13-14 (ESV)*

Paul said about our relationship with Christ, *"We were buried therefore with him by baptism into death, in order that, just as Christ was raised from the dead by the glory of the Father, we too might walk in newness of life." - Romans 6:4 (ESV)*

In John 10:10 Jesus compared Himself as a shepherd to a thief. The same could be said of the parasites in our life what Jesus said of the thief: *"The thief comes only to steal and kill and destroy. I came that they may have life and have it abundantly." - John 10:10 (ESV)*

For those who seek after God, there is a reward. According to Hebrews 11:6, it is impossible to walk in a way that pleases God without believing that He is a God who rewards those who seek Him. *"And without faith it is impossible to please him, for whoever would draw near to God must believe that he exists and that he rewards those who seek him.*" If you make Christ your priority, everything else in your walk will gain new life. If you want your life to improve, seek Christ. If you want your marriage to improve, seek Christ. If you want your relationships to improve, seek life in Christ. In Christ there is a wellspring of abundant life that never runs dry. Unlike the parasite that sucks the life out of you, Christ will add vitality to every area of life in which you make Him the priority.

The danger with parasites as your priority is that once a parasite sucks the life out of you, you will find that there is no life in it.

In the 1981 classic film *Chariots of Fire,* Eric Liddell's rival Harold Abrams, reflects on the most important race of his life, which is just hours away. Unlike Abrams, Liddell is an incredible runner, but racing is not his priority. His life is defined by his walk with God. For Abrams, winning is all he has. In a dramatic scene in which he reflects on the race to come, Abrams offers a chilling assessment, "I will raise my eyes and look down that corridor; 4 feet wide, with 10 lonely seconds to justify my whole existence. But will I? I've known the fear of losing, but now I am almost too frightened to win."

What is it that you believe justifies your whole existence? If it is a parasite, you are probably too afraid to win. Like Abrams, you know once you obtain it, there will be nothing left.

Abrams wins the race, and the subsequent scene shows him in celebration in a local pub. The scene cuts away and comes back to Abrams, much later, sitting alone in the same bar. He won the race that he thought justified his existence, and he gave all to it. Alone in the pub, the inevitable emptiness he feared sets in.

Abrams sought life in winning a race. Instead, he found that in the end the race was a parasite. It was a lie in his right hand. He had fashioned for himself an idol in his mind and in his heart that he thought would give him life. He made winning the race his priority. Yet, after pouring all of his life into his idol, he found it empty. After a parasite sucks the life out of you, you will find that there is no life in it.

———————

The right priority gives us the right perspective. In Matthew 13 Jesus tells two parables to illustrate what happens to those who focus on His Kingdom as a priority.

"The kingdom of heaven is like treasure hidden in a field, which a man found and covered up. Then in his joy he goes and sells all that he has and buys that field."

"Again, the kingdom of heaven is like a merchant in search of fine pearls, who, on finding one pearl of great value, went and sold all that he had and bought it." - Matthew 13:44-46 (ESV)

It would be an epiphany moment for you to put down the leg end of the chair and get those four or five things that you think are priority out of your face and focus. When the lion tamer puts up the leg end of the chair, it distracts the lion and he forgets that, with one swat, the lion tamer loses his face. Imagine how far you could go if your walk with God became priority.

If the first thing is a wellspring, like the people Jesus illustrated in the parables, we need to bring everything to that one thing. Paul describes it like this, "*So, whether you eat or drink, or whatever you do, do all to the glory of God.*" *- 1 Corinthians 10:31 (ESV)*

The walk doesn't change some things, it changes everything. Your walk with God is about not only attending church or reading the Bible; the walk is about business, family, study, community, everything for the glory of God. If you can't do it to the glory of God, it is a parasite to you, not a wellspring.

If the first thing is the wrong thing, nothing changes.

My biggest fear as a pastor is that people enjoy my sermons, but never change. If you read this book and love it, even talk about how much you have learned from it, it may boost my ego, but it is an epic failure if your life is not changed.

You can't go anywhere by going only part of the way. Buying flowery shorts, a floppy hat, and a map of Florida does nothing to change where you are. If you want to go to Florida, you can't just dress like you're there, you must go.

In James 1:22-25 we have a comedic but tragic scene that takes place far too often with people of great intentions.

"But be doers of the word, and not hearers only, deceiving yourselves. For if anyone is a hearer of the word and not a doer, he is like a man who looks intently at his natural face in a mirror. For

he looks at himself and goes away and at once forgets what he was like. But the one who looks into the perfect law, the law of liberty, and perseveres, being no hearer who forgets but a doer who acts, he will be blessed in his doing." - James 1:22-25 (ESV)

Here is the scene James describes. It is you getting out of the bed after a long night of sleep. I'm not really sure what goes on while you sleep, but I do know that after several hours of it you are a total wreck. Your hair is matted and sticking up in odd places. There are creases on your face and on your skin from folds in the sheets. I'm not sure about the biology of it all, but wow, what happens to your breath during the night?

The picture James offers is as if you wake up, walk from the bed to the mirror, take a long look at your disheveled self and without making a single adjustment to your appearance, say, "I'm good."

You make no improvements. You make no changes. The mirror is faithful in showing you the problems, but you don't address them. You just go on in your PJ's about your day. I think James shopped at Wal-Mart. You've probably seen those PJ people shopping there too.

We have too many people who know the truth, but stay in their PJ's all day. It is time to make a change.

Lip service is not life change.

Walking with God requires more than lip service, it requires life change. If we walk with God, there will be a sense of moral urgency about us.

"Besides this you know the time, that the hour has come for you to wake from sleep. For salvation is nearer to us now than when we first believed. The night is far gone; the day is at hand. So then let us cast off the works of darkness and put on the armor of light. Let us walk properly as in the daytime, not in orgies and drunkenness, not in sexual immorality and sensuality, not in quarreling and jealousy. But put on the Lord Jesus Christ, and make no provision for the flesh, to gratify its desires." - Romans 13:11-14 (ESV)

If you want to get something clean, invite someone over. It is amazing how many things I put off that I will accomplish with a sense of urgency when we invite our extended family over. We moved into a new house in July but did not get some things done until late November. Why? The family was coming over for Thanksgiving.

Imagine Jesus was coming to your house for dinner tomorrow night at 7. I would think there would be a real sense of urgency in cleaning up some things around your home before the Master shows up.

If we walk with God, His moral attributes demand change in our lives. Read the words of Moses as he addressed the people about the urgency of change if they desired to walk with God:

And now, Israel, what does the LORD your God require of you, but to fear the LORD your God, to walk in all his ways, to love him, to serve the LORD your God with all your heart and with all your soul, and to keep the commandments and statutes of the LORD, which I am commanding you today for your good?

Behold, to the LORD your God belong heaven and the heaven of heavens, the earth with all that is in it. Yet the LORD set his heart in love on your fathers and chose their offspring after them, you above all peoples, as you are this day. Circumcise therefore the foreskin of your heart, and be no longer stubborn. For the LORD your God is God of gods and Lord of lords, the great, the mighty, and the awesome God, who is not partial and takes no bribe. He executes justice for the fatherless and the widow, and loves the sojourner, giving him food and clothing. Love the sojourner, therefore, for you were sojourners in the land of Egypt. You shall fear the LORD your God. You shall serve him and hold fast to him, and by his name you shall swear. He is your praise. He is your God, who has done for you these great and terrifying things that your eyes have seen. Your fathers went down to Egypt seventy persons, and now the LORD your God has made you as numerous as the stars of heaven. - Deuteronomy 10:12-22 (ESV)

Not only do God's moral attributes demand that we change, but His moral excellence deserves it. It is not just who God is that brings about urgent change in our lives, but it is also the way God is. The longer we are with a person and the deeper the relationship grows, it is interesting how characteristics of the other person begin to influence us. It is especially true of people we admire. The longer we are with them, the more we try to pattern our lives after theirs.

In Galatians 5:19-24 Paul contrasts two ways of living. He contrasts life in the flesh with life in the Spirit. Life in the flesh is doing what you want to do. Life in the Spirit is doing what God wants you to do.

"Now the works of the flesh are evident: sexual immorality, impurity, sensuality, idolatry, sorcery, enmity, strife, jealousy, fits of anger, rivalries, dissensions, divisions, envy, drunkenness, orgies, and things like these. I warn you, as I warned you before, that those who do such things will not inherit the kingdom of God. But the fruit of the Spirit is love, joy, peace, patience, kindness, goodness, faithfulness, gentleness, self-control; against such things there is no law. And those who belong to Christ Jesus have crucified the flesh with its passions and desires." - Galatians 5:19-24 (ESV)

If there is no moral change in us, the passage makes it clear - we shouldn't be deceived into thinking that we will inherit the kingdom of God. *Lip service is not life change.*

Yet, for those who walk in the Spirit, they begin to do things the way God does things. The ways of God become their walk. They live out His Word and exhibit His attributes in everything they do. You can tell when a person has spent time with God. There is something very different about them.

If your first thing is your walk with the Lord, nothing stays the same.

In 2 Chronicles 34:3 we read the story of a young king who found the power of the right priority.

"Josiah was eight years old when he began to reign, and he reigned thirty-one years in Jerusalem. And he did what was right in the eyes of the LORD, and walked in the ways of David his father; and he did not turn aside to the right hand or to the left. For in the eighth year of his reign, while he was yet a boy, he began to seek the God of David his father, and in the twelfth year he began to purge Judah and Jerusalem of the high places, the Asherim, and the carved and the metal images." - 2 Chronicles 34:1-3 (ESV)

When our kids are eight years old, we want them to cut straight and color in the lines. When Josiah was eight, he became king. Now that's expecting more from your kids!

At 16 he made a decision that was a game changer. For the next four years of his life, he invested himself in seeking God. He got the leg end of the chair out of his face and walked with focus. What is the result? He went much further than the kings before him.

At age 20, 12 years after becoming king, Josiah morally reformed his nation. He brought about urgent change. We have very low spiritual expectations for our teens. As a result, they don't go very far.

We hope they will be serious about seeking God, but when they don't, we are not surprised. We are not surprised that when they are 20, they are absorbed into the culture instead of becoming distinct from it. Yet Josiah, because he had the right priority, didn't become like the culture, he reformed it.

Our students are capable of much more than we expect. So are their parents. So is their church. The problem is that we have the leg end of the chair in front of our faces. We are potentially powerful, but paralyzed by not knowing what to do next. Even a powerful creature out of focus is ineffective. The problem is lack of priority.

The first thing determines everything. Had Josiah made cultural reform his priority, he would have failed. Reforming the nation is an incredible vision and an even more incredible task. But reform is not what God called Josiah ultimately to do. Had Josiah made winning wars his priority, that is certainly the business of kings, but it was not what God had ultimately called him to do. I am sure, as king, Josiah had a lot of demands on his time. I'm sure teen kings are busy. But Josiah got the leg end of the chair out of his face, and he sought God as his priority. He did the one thing God has ultimately, only called us to do - walk in a way that pleases Him. Priority is powerful.

Progress

Finally, then, brothers, we ask and urge you in the Lord Jesus, that as you received from us how you ought to live and to please God, just as you are doing, and that you do so more and more.
- 1 Thessalonians 4:8 (ESV)

In 1 Thessalonians 4 Paul encourages a struggling group of Christians to continue making progress. He says,

Finally, then, brothers, we ask and urge you in the Lord Jesus, that as you received from us how you ought to walk and to please God, just as you are doing, that you do so more and more. ² For you know what instructions we gave you through the Lord Jesus. ³ For this is the will of God, your sanctification: that you abstain from sexual immorality; ⁴ that each one of you know how to control his own body in holiness and honor, ⁵ not in the passion of lust like the Gentiles who do not know God; ⁶ that no one transgress and wrong his brother in this matter, because the Lord is an avenger in all these things, as we told you beforehand and solemnly warned you. ⁷ For God has not called us for impurity, but in holiness. ⁸ Therefore whoever disregards this, disregards not man but God, who gives his Holy Spirit to you." - 1 Thessalonians 4:1–8 (ESV)

In verse 3 Paul uses a very important word: *sanctification*. What does the word *sanctification* mean? *Sanctification* describes two things God does in our lives when He saves us: 1) He sets us apart as His own and 2) He cleans up our walk. You may be more familiar with the word *holy*. The words *sanctification* and *holy* are closely related. If *sanctification* is the process then *holiness* is the result.

When we think of someone who is holy, we usually think of how moral they are. While this may be true, holiness not only describes the way one acts; holiness describes what something is. The way Paul is using the word *sanctification* is to describe the process of getting who we are in Christ to agree with what we do.

At its heart, the word *holy* means that God has selected something to be His. In the Bible, God took many things to be His own and made them holy. It wasn't just people who were made holy, but also animals, material, utensils, cups - even the ground could be made holy (Exo. 3:5). Once God made it His own, all of the defilements were removed. Once something became God's, it could never be used in the same way again.

If this is the case with our lives, we must ask two questions at this point:[18] How thoroughly will I be cleaned up and how long will it take? Let's address the issue of thoroughness first.

Should we expect to one day reach perfection? Can a person somehow reach a status where every sermon he has ever heard, every Scripture he has ever read, every prayer he has ever prayed suddenly converge and the person no longer has a bad thought or sinful desire? Will temptation one day be something ...

The good news is "yes." The not so good news . . . it's not going to happen in this life, we will have to die first.

One day, after the resurrection, we will be made perfect in Christ (1 John 3:2). Yet the Bible indicates that until that time, we will continue to struggle with sinful desires and temptations (1 John 1, Rom. 7, James 1:14-15). As holy as we would think Paul to be, he admitted in Philippians 3:12, "*Not that I have already obtained this or am already perfect, but I press on to make it my own, because Christ Jesus has made me his own.*" This is an important statement as it reveals that, for Paul, there was a real sense of expectation of progress in sanctification in his life.

The church makes a big mistake if there is acceptance without expectation. Churches are to be forgiving communities where people experience God's grace, but churches should also be expectant communities providing a positive pressure for people to progress in sanctification.

When a woman caught in the act of adultery was brought to Jesus in John 8, Jesus began to draw in the dirt. As He scratched out a message in the dirt, Jesus issued a piercing challenge to her accusers: "Let him who is without sin among you, cast the first stone at her." One by one, as conviction seemed to grow in them, all of her accusers left. In Christ, she found acceptance. But in Christ, she also found expectation. Jesus shows us the balance in His conversation with her when he says in verse 11, "*Neither do I*

condemn you (acceptance); go, and from now on sin no more
(expectation).

Even though we do not expect to reach perfection in this life, there should still be in us, as God's holy people, an expectation of progress. There may not be a moment of instantaneous change that will remove every sinful thought from our mind, but there is a sense in which our minds are being cleansed in Christ. Notice what Paul says in 1 Thessalonians 4:1. He uses the words "more and more" to describe the progress they are making. There should be a sense that, in our lives, we may not be perfect, but "more and more" who we are in Christ is agreeing with what we do.

So the next question is, "How long will this take?" There are some things in our lives that seem to be crippling habits, addictive tendencies, and desires too strong to manage. We desperately want these things to be a part of our distant past, but we still seem to constantly contend with them. We are frustrated because instead of "more and more," it seems that we are progressing "less and less," if at all.

One afternoon, while driving down a major highway, I passed a man who was walking. He was dressed in military fatigues and carrying a large American flag. I noticed him, but moved on quickly and gave it very little thought.

Two days later I saw the same man standing with his American flag, surrounded by a small crowd of people at a street corner in a different town. This time, he was at least 15 miles away from where I had seen him before. That weekend I was hosting a retreat for a group of men at a facility located at the summit of a mountain. As I left the retreat center that Saturday afternoon, guess whom I saw. I saw the same man wearing military fatigues, carrying the same flag, walking down the other side of the mountain. He was now 30+ miles from where I had first seen him and 3,000 feet in elevation above the town where I had seen him just a day or so before.

That's progress!

After doing some research, I found out that the man's name is Mac McQuown and he is on a journey to bring awareness to the needs of U.S. military veterans. He is doing so by visiting the capital buildings of all 50 states. As of the day I last saw him, Mac had completed more than 2,800 miles of a walk that will take him at least 6 years to finish.

Like Mac's journey, the Christian life is very pedestrian. It is about steady progress. The Christian walk is also, like Mac's walk, not about going fast, but about going far.

As much as we enjoy the miracle stories in which someone is drastically and radically changed, it is important to understand that the Christian life is not so much about miracle moments as it is about progress. True, some people have certain desires in their lives seemingly, instantaneously sanctified. I know people who have had their desire for alcohol or drugs completely taken away. I praise the Lord for His grace in this. Without divine intervention, I don't see any hope of these people succeeding in their walk. Taking those desires away is not only an act of sanctification, it is an act of healing. In the same way Jesus can make a lame man walk, He can take away the desire of a hardened alcoholic for another drink.

As incredible as these experiences may be, it is important to note that they are rare. It is also important to note that even though certain desires are taken away, these same people are still left to walk along seeking sanctification with other desires and temptations that may be a real struggle for them.

I pray for certain things in my life to happen quickly, but they rarely do. The interest God has in my life has less to do with miracles and more to do with my progress in the mundane. There is nothing more mundane than walking. Sanctification is about steady progress. It is not about majoring on what happened to me "one incredible day" as much as it is about the way I am thinking and behaving EVERYDAY. Just keep moving forward. My goal is to be further along today than yesterday, and further long tomorrow than I am today. Like McQuown, a few days of consistent progress goes a long way.

The Biblical metaphor of *walking* is powerful because it teaches us not only about the pace, but it also reveals to us something critical about progress.

Significant progress is made one step at a time.

Mac McQuown will only be able to accomplish a 6-year walk one way: one step at a time. Sanctification is a process of progress. It is not an instantaneous gift, nor is it the achievement of the super-spiritual. Sanctification is the journey of learning how your walk needs to conform to Christ's walk. It is about getting your thoughts, habits, and attitudes to agree with the death, burial, and resurrection of Christ. It is about getting what you do to reflect what Christ has done for you. The only way to succeed in sanctification is one step at a time.

My problem is I am way too passive. I want to pray away my sinful tendencies without having to take intentional steps in the right direction. Some things in my life I want to hitch hike past, but instead of picking me up and bypassing a necessary part of the journey, God just leaves me to walk it out.

The problem is that God is working, but I am not responding. We are expected to respond to God's work and to God's Word. We need an intentional plan for progress in our walk. By working through Paul's words in 1 Thessalonians 4:1-8, I want to show you how to make significant progress, one step at a time. To help you remember these ideas, I want to use the acronym STEP as a guide. The acronym will look like this:

Study

Think

Exchange

Proceed

_____

S - Study

Sources are critical to study. Where do you get your information? You can't make good decisions based on bad information. You must study the right sources. For those who walk with Christ, there are three sources of study: *the Word of God*, *the Spirit of God*, and *the people of God*. Let's talk first about the Word of God as a source.

Paul says in 1 Thessalonians 4:2, *"For you know what instructions we gave you through the Lord Jesus."* How do we know what is right? We know because it has been revealed to us in the Word of God, in the Bible. The Bible is the authority for behavior in the Christian life. If we are to make progress in sanctification we do not trust intuition or emotion. We make progress by study, through investigation of the Word of God.

Something that feels right may make me immediately happy, but it may disagree with the Word of God. I may have a gut feeling about something and be thoroughly convinced in my own mind that it is the right thing to do. The Bible warns us about trusting our gut instincts or even favorable feelings by saying, *"There is a way that seems right to a man, but its end is the way to death."* - *Proverbs 14:12* (ESV)

Only by investing time and energy into reading and studying the Bible will I learn what God expects of me. Bible study is also very pedestrian. There are no shortcuts, and there is no hitch hiking. Bible study is slow and steady, one step at a time. But the pace is not as critical as the progress. Paul says in 1 Thess. 4:1 we ought to walk and please God. If I am to please God, I must know what God has said.

As we are grounded in the Word of God we will become more sensitive to the Spirit of God. The Spirit of God, in agreement with the Word of God, brings two things into our lives that are critical to progress - *illumination* and *conviction*.

There is no doubt that the Bible can be difficult to understand. There is somewhat of an academic process to interpreting Scripture as one investigates the meaning of words and historical contexts. Paul instructed Pastor Timothy in 2 Timothy 2:15 to "rightly handle" the Word of God.

But there must be more than a faithful academic process to Bible study. Unless the Word of God becomes personal to us and we become willing to obey it, the academic part of studying the Bible may be intellectually stimulating, but it will be spiritually fruitless. This is where the Spirit's work of illumination is critical.

The idea of illumination describes the Holy Spirit's work of doing two things as we study Scripture. He helps us not only to understand the Word of God, but to receive it. The Bible says in 1 Cor. 2:10-14,

> *These things God has revealed to us through the Spirit. For the Spirit searches everything, even the depths of God. For who knows a person's thoughts except the spirit of that person, which is in him? So also no one comprehends the thoughts of God except the Spirit of God. Now we have received not the spirit of the world, but the Spirit who is from God, that **we***

might understand the things freely given us by God. And we impart this in words not taught by human wisdom but taught by the Spirit, interpreting spiritual truths to those who are spiritual.

The natural person does not accept the things of the Spirit of God, for they are folly to him, and he is not able to understand them because they are spiritually discerned.

The second thing the Spirit does in our lives that helps us progress through study is He brings conviction. *Conviction is the work of the Word and the Spirit to redeem the conscience.* The more we are in the Word of God, the more our attitudes will begin to change toward things that we once did with very little trouble to our conscience. As the Spirit instructs our conscience through the Word, slowly, over time, these same things we did with little thought just don't feel right, and they are not as desirable as they once were. There is a deeper sense of shame and disgrace in us, even though no one else my know what we are doing. This is the Spirit's work of conviction in the life of the redeemed.

Conviction is important to sanctification because it moves us from the negative motive of the fear of being caught to the positive one of desiring to please God.

As we study the Word of God and become more sensitive to the Spirit of God, we must also submit ourselves to the people of God. If we are to make progress, we need the positive pressure of a believing community that accepts us, but also expects us to change.

As discussed previously, sanctification describes how God sets us apart and cleans us up. This process will require separation in our lives. There may be some relationships and some sources that will require some distance. Who are the negative influences in your life that impede your progress? It is time to distance yourself from them.

In 1 Thessalonians 4 Paul chooses the example of sexual immorality as an area in which his readers need to make progress in pleasing the Lord more and more. Coming out of a thoroughly godless culture, these new Christians in the first century make up a distinct minority when compared to the behaviors and thoughts of the people surrounding them. Things that were sexually prevalent, acceptable, expected, and even encouraged in the Thessalonian culture are now found to be displeasing to God.[19] If they were to make progress in this behavior, they needed a new community as a source of information.

Paul says that their new behavior is *"not in the passion of lust like the Gentiles who do not know God."* - *1 Thessalonians 4:5 (ESV)*

Simply stated, if you are to make progress, you can't put yourself in a position to be influenced by people who take pleasure in things that do not please God. Furthermore, you can't expect that these people would influence you to take the right steps because they do not know God. If they do not know God, it should be no surprise to you then that they think, advise, encourage, and act as they do.

In Colossians 1:10 Paul teaches that increasing in our knowledge of the Lord is critical to our walk. *"So as to walk in a manner worthy of the Lord, fully pleasing to him, bearing fruit in every good work and increasing in the knowledge of God." - Colossians 1:10 (ESV)*

Christians are not to take moral cues from people who do not know the Lord.

If you are to make sanctified progress, you can't take your fashion cues from people who don't know the Lord. You shouldn't share things on *Facebook* as people do who don't know the Lord. You shouldn't talk, think, or joke like people who don't know the Lord. You shouldn't spend your time or our money like people who don't know the Lord. You shouldn't pattern your time on the weekends like people who do not know the Lord.

Kanye and Kim are not good guides for your steps. Keeping up with the Kardashians will not help you progress in Christ-likeness. Whether on TV, radio, magazines, or books; even if it is your best friend, to make progress you need to recognize and distance yourself from ungodly sources.

Changing communities is an incredible challenge. Creating distance from ungodly sources will not come without pressure. You do not have to be unkind or unfriendly, but you do sometimes need new friends. This is where connecting with God's people becomes critical.

If you want to make progress, you need to be submitted to a Spirit-filled group of people who know the Lord, who are serious about salvation and sanctification, and take His Word seriously. You are not looking for a group of perfect people, but you are looking for a group of people who are walking in the right direction. The church is not about perfection, but rather pressure toward progress. You can't walk alone (Gen. 2:18).

It is important to say at this point that it is not enough to simply go to church. You and I need to submit ourselves to a church. We need to be under the authority of a group of people who are led by the Spirit and grounded in God's Word.

In the church you should find people who are a step ahead. Seek out the people who are where you want to be. Their children are older than yours. They have been married longer than you. When it comes to church, don't simply seek out people who are like you, but also connect with people who *were* where you *are*. These people will become great sources of information and encouragement for your walk.

T - *Think*

Paul writes in 1 Thessalonians 4:3 - 6, "*For this is the will of God, your sanctification: that you abstain from sexual immorality; that each one of you know how to control his own body in holiness and honor, not in the passion of lust like the Gentiles who do not know God; that no one transgress and wrong his brother in this matter, because the Lord is an avenger in all these things, as we told you beforehand and solemnly warned you.*"

Central to this part of the passage is the word *know*. We have already seen how we need to separate ourselves from allowing people who do not know the Lord to influence the way we think, but there is also something else we need to know. We need to know how to control our bodies in holiness and honor.

There are two things we need to think about. We have discussed the word *holiness*. It is obvious then that to control our bodies in holiness means that we need to think about how our actions will affect our relationship with the Lord.

The word *honor* means that we need to think about how our actions will affect our relationships with other people.

How do we think of our actions in relation to God? The word *confess* is helpful here. *Confess* means "to agree." Confessing sin is not simply saying to God, "Forgive me of all of my sin." That statement sounds religious, but it is heartless.

What if someone cheats on his spouse and simply requests, "Please forgive me of all I have done to you." That person then gives his devastated spouse a hug, goes to the kitchen, fixes a snack, and then sits down on the couch and watches TV. Even though the request is made, it has no heart. Forgiveness and reconciliation are not automatic because there is an obvious lack of agreement.

So what if that person, realizing the situation was no better, then said, "I'm sorry I have made you upset, please forgive me." Again, another heartless request that doesn't really agree with the gravity of the situation. The problem is not that this person has upset his spouse, the problem is that he has betrayed trust, he has broken a covenant, he has committed an act of deception, and he has emotionally and physically given to someone else something that was devoted to his spouse. Wouldn't you agree that saying you are sorry is not the same as saying what you've done? If there is to be any hope of progress, there must first be agreement.

In the Greek, the word translated "sexual immorality" is *porneia*. It is the word from which we derive "pornography." Yet, it is not a word in Greek reserved only for explicit images. *Porneia* is a vile word that covers the gambit of sexual sin. There is nothing beautiful about it. In Greek, *Porneia* is a filthy word that describes a filthy thing. *Filthy words are the native tongue of true confession.*

Confession sounds filthy because in true confession one agrees with God about the sin that has been committed to the point that he is willing to name it to the depth of what it is. Until you can agree with a holy God that your sin is filthy and you can understand what it does to your relationship with Him, there is no real confession. If it is porneia, call it porneia. Ask God to forgive you of porneia. Don't just ask God mechanically to simply "forgive me of all my sin." Name it.

To have a heart for God before we act will help us progress in holiness. Confession is one thing, but to realize the gravity of our actions before we proceed is knowing how to control our bodies in holiness. We need to think about how our actions will affect our relationship with God. That is holiness.

In "honor", we need to also think about how our actions will affect our relationships with others. We said in the *S-Study* step that we need to be submitted to a group of Spirit-led people who know the Lord and take His Word seriously. We have also discussed how these people should meet us with not only acceptance but expectation. If we are to make progress, we need not only some thought about how our sin affects our relationship with the Lord, but also how sin affects our relationships with all people, but especially with these people.

Paul takes the sin of porneia a step further. It is not only a sin before God, but it is a sin against the brethren. He says in verse 6, "*that no one transgress and wrong his brother in this matter.*"

Our culture promotes the idea of the rugged individualist. What one chooses to do is one's own business. As long as what one does brings no harm or infringes on someone else's rights, then it is believed that his actions have no impact on the surrounding community.

The Biblical ethic is much different. Sin is never an individual matter; it is always something that should be considered as an act that impacts a community.

Even though Paul has the entire scope of sexual sin in sight, his choice to use the word *porneia* is interesting in light of the prevalence of pornography in our culture. It is not hard to see the damage that adultery brings to marriage and families, but how does pornography impact community?

Our culture would say it is no one else's business if someone wants to surf the internet and visit a porn sight. That is the choice of the individual. Yet, Paul has already warned us that we should not take our moral cues from those who do not know God. Furthermore, research shows that the idea that pornography is a private sin could not be further from the truth.

Morality in Media, a leading national organization for public education and for the opposition of pornography and the promotion of decency in the the media since 1962, reports that pornography has a deep impact on mental health, marriage, children, and culture. Pornography has been shown to promote violence in teens, child abuse, and it fuels a rampant underground sex-trade industry. Pornography has been shown to promote criminal behavior as it can actually deceive men into believing that women do not suffer from rape and may even enjoy it. For married couples, pornography undermines sexual health and negatively impacts the way one views and values his or her spouse.[20]

Especially for the Christian, one cannot view pornography as a private matter. The people on the screen or in the magazine are someone's children. That woman is someone's daughter. Behind the image is a destroyed family. How can we walk with Christ and take pleasure out of something that requires someone else's life and family to be so twisted? There is no honor in pornography.

Pornography amongst God's people destroys not only the power of the church but its integrity. If the public scandal of pornography in the church is not embarrassing enough, it is devastating to the power of God the church should be experiencing together. A church filled with men and women participating in pornography is a far cry from the church that Christ set as a precedent in the Book of Acts. Pornography in the church diminishes the glory of God in His people and ultimately undermines our witness before the world.

This idea of the impact of sin on community is not exclusive to pornography. Every sin somehow betrays the trust and the purity of community. If you want to take the right step, be sure to THINK how your actions will impact your relationship with God and with others. Thinking helps us to realize that a sin is not wrong only if we are caught; sin does damage to our relationship with God and with others, even if no one ever knows what we have done.

E - Exchange

We need to exchange doing wrong for doing right. To make progress, we need to exchange negative behaviors for positive ones. Paul tells us not only to abstain from sexual immorality, but *"that each one of you know how to control his own body in holiness and honor." - 1 Thess. 4:4* (ESV)

Quitting is not changing. Jesus tells a story in Matthew 12 of a man who emptied his life of an unclean spirit, but failed to replace the resulting void in his life with something clean. The man ends up worse than he was at first.

"When the unclean spirit has gone out of a person, it passes through waterless places seeking rest, but finds none. Then it says, 'I

will return to my house from which I came.' And when it comes, it finds the house empty, swept, and put in order. Then it goes and brings with it seven other spirits more evil than itself, and they enter and dwell there, and the last state of that person is worse than the first. So also will it be with this evil generation." - Matthew 12:43-45 (ESV)

In Ephesians 4:17-32 Paul teaches that the key to dealing with the old self with its corrupt habits and desires is to learn Christ. He speaks of putting off and putting on. The thief doesn't just stop stealing; he learns to do honest work (Eph. 4:28) and to share with those who have need. We don't just refrain from cursing and corrupt speech, but we learn to speak in ways that build people up and impart grace to the hearer (Eph. 4:29).

When it comes to sexual immorality, Paul exhorts the reader not only to abstain, but to learn how to control his body in holiness and honor. Whereas those who do not know God are characterized by unbridled passion and lust, Christians are to be characterized by control. This does not mean that Christians will not have just as strong desires as people who do not know the Lord. The difference is not desire; the difference is control.

The word *control* is interesting in that it can also be translated "acquire" or "to gain mastery over" something. This may not be an easy task, but it is necessary. Progress is not passive. There is denial and sacrifice. There will be times of incredible frustration. It is a process of unlearning and re-learning. Control is about de-habit and re-habit. For our patriot walker Mac McQuown, having the plan and desire to walk over a mountain is one thing; pushing through each breathless step is quite another.

P - Proceed

Proceeding is about taking the next step for the right reason. Even if we go the right way, if we go for the wrong reason, we will find that soon our motivation will run dry and we will not get very far. Mac McQuown has a cause that will keep him walking through 50 states. We need a reason worthy enough to keep us walking.

The walk will require change. There are lots of reasons people make changes. Some are motivated by personal ambition. They are extremely driven, they are frustrated with their current condition, and they are determined to work at it as hard as they possibly can.

Personal ambition may take you far, but not far enough. What if you don't get the results you are seeking? What if you find that it is too difficult? What if you find that you don't have the will power to pull it off?

Perhaps you have the will power and the determination, but what if your walk ends in vanity? What if you end up a more improved version of yourself, but you are still out of pace with Christ? Personal ambition is not a sufficient reason to keep you walking as far as you need to go.

Some people are motivated by the pressure of their peers. The reasons here may vary from negative ones, like family crisis or the threat of loss, to positive ones, like a group of people supporting you for a cause. Without serious changes, you may lose your job or perhaps even your family. For a time it looks like you have taken some drastic steps of progress, but as soon as you seem to reach a sense of equilibrium, when the pressure is off, you regress instead of continue to progress. Why is this the case?

Most of the time we make surface, environmental changes rather than core corrections. Our motivating factor is to keep our jobs, to appease our wives, to satisfy the group, but until we change who we actually are, we will not get far with what we actually do. If we change for the sake of the group, it's all external; there's nothing really being sanctified internally.

So what is the real reason we should proceed? In 1 Thessalonians 4:6-8 Paul ends the paragraph by saying that we ultimately do what we do, *"because the Lord is an avenger in all these things, as we told you beforehand and solemnly warned you. For God has not called us for impurity, but in holiness. Therefore whoever disregards this, disregards not man, but God who gives His Holy Spirit to you."*

We can summarize Paul's words here with this thought: ultimately, the gospel is the only sufficient reason that will help us make long, sustained progress in sanctification. Only in the gospel do we find the sufficient motive and power to change. Knowing Christ and living out His gospel is the only real motive that will keep us walking further.

The gospel gives us reason to proceed with a reverent sense of fear. We serve a loving and joyous God, but we should never lose sight of the fact that He is an avenger. He is jealous for His name. He is jealous for His people. He is a righteous judge. The Lord *accepts* us for the sake of His Son, but there is a very real *expectation* that we bear fruit (Isaiah 5:1-7, Matthew 7:15-20).

The gospel gives us reason to proceed with a sense of call. Mac McQuown is walking for a worthy cause. Christians do not have only a cause, but a call. Paul says that God has not called us to impurity, but to holiness. Our walk should please Him.

A wise pastor gave me some great wisdom early on in my ministry. He said, "Brian, sometimes all you're going to have is your call." I didn't really understand what he meant at the time, but, looking back now, being much further down the path, I know exactly what he meant.

There are a lot of great reasons I do what I do. I love people, but there have been times when there were people who really didn't love me. I love visiting families who have just birthed a new son or daughter into the world. But I have also had to stand with some families and grieve with them over the tragic loss of a newborn. I love to see the church grow. I struggle when it doesn't.

Sometimes you will not have approval. Sometimes you will not have results. Sometimes you will not have all the answers. Sometimes all you have is your call. To know that God has called us to walk with Him will carry us through any circumstances we must endure. Your higher call to live for Christ will carry you far.

The gospel gives us reason to proceed with authority. Paul says that "*whoever disregards this, disregards not man, but God.*" To walk with God means that we do not just read the Bible, but we read it so that we may do what it says. We take the Bible not to be the mere writings of men, but to be inspired by God.

The gospel gives us reason to proceed with power. If I am going to progress, I need help. There have been plenty of moments in my walk in which I have tried and failed. The good news is that God has not left us without help. Paul says that it is God, "who gives his Holy Spirit to you." In John 16:7 Jesus said that it would be an advantage to us that He go away so that He could send us a helper. He was speaking of the Holy Spirit. As we discussed previously, the Holy Spirit is a critical source, not only of information, but also of strength for our walk.

In every decision and action, think **STEP**. *Study* - what are my sources? Am I making decisions based on the Word of God, led by the Spirit of God, seeking the counsel of the people of God? *Think* - Am I taking the next step, having in mind how it will affect my relationship with God (in holiness) and with His people (in honor)? *Exchange* - quitting is not changing. I need to not only stop doing wrong, but I need to start doing what is right. *Proceed* - what is my reason for walking? I may be moving in the right direction, but if it is not for the right reason, I will not get very far. We need something below the surface. We walk for the sake of Christ and the gospel.

Plan

For to this you have been called, because Christ also suffered for you, leaving you an example, so that you might follow in his steps. - 1 Peter 2:21 (ESV)

Do you want to go faster or further? If you've read this book to this point, no doubt your choice is to go further. One final question: What's your plan? If you want to walk far, you must have a plan.

Some of us were naturally built for endurance. I'm not one of those people. I like all kinds of sports and consider myself fairly athletic. But my body was built more for sports that are measured in quarters, halves, and won by scoring points. Sports that are measured in meters - not my thing.

As I was approaching age 41, some friends challenged me to do something I had never considered doing before: run a triathlon. The term "run a triathlon" is misleading, because you also swim and bike a triathlon. A triathlon is not merely one distance event, but three: swim, then bike, then run. No one asked me to do this at age 18, or perhaps even 25. Instead my friends hit me up at my mid-life to do an endurance race. Let the crisis begin.

I should clarify. This was no Ironman event. The Ironman triathlons are comprised of a 2.4-mile open water swim, followed by a 112-mile bike ride, capped off by a full 26.2-mile marathon. The event I entered is called a sprint triathlon. The word "sprint" is a bit misleading because for me it does not describe the speed as much as it does the shortened distance. Instead of 2.4, 112, and 26.2, we are talking 300m, 12, and 2. Even at that distance, it was further than I've ever tried to go before.

Agreeing to the event required a change in my routine. It required me to get out of the bed earlier and run. Every few runs I tried to push myself further. To my running I then added swimming.

I trained my body by eating better. I tried to prepare my mind by reading as much as I could from people who compete often in triathlons. I had to not only plan my training routine leading up to the race, but I also had to plan my strategy for the race. I had one goal: Finish without stopping.

I'm happy to report - Mission accomplished! It wasn't pretty, but, because of my pre-race plan, I was able to do something I was not previously able to do. I planned to go further than I had ever been before and I did it. Without several weeks of training and planning, I had no chance.

In the opening chapter of the book, "Why Walk" I offered several areas of life in which the things and the people we influence the most need us not to go faster, but to go further. Now that we have unpacked that thought throughout this book, I would add another thought to the equation. You don't need to just go further; you need to finish. You need to finish without stopping.

So what's your plan for making it to the finish line?

In one of his final communications to his apprentice Timothy, Paul says, "*I have fought the good fight, I have finished the race, I have kept the faith.*" - *2 Timothy 4:7 (ESV)*

Can you imagine what it must be like to be at the end of your life and be satisfied, not that you did a lot, but that you did it all? You finished without stopping. You didn't just go further, but you went as far as you were supposed to go.

Think of how much we are doing in the busy pace of our lives and how categorically unsatisfied we are with all of it. Do a simple *Google* search of the words "unsatisfied" and "Americans" and you will see poll upon poll citing statistics that we are unsatisfied with everything from the performance of politicians, to our jobs, from our marriages, to our money. We are extremely busy with being dissatisfied.

The only way you can possibly be satisfied with the result of a race is to be satisfied with where you are during the race. My goal in the triathlon was not to run up front. My goal was to simply keep running. I wanted to finish. While I was in the pool, I kept swimming. While I was on the bike, I kept peddling. When it came to the run, I could not feel much from the knee down, but I kept running. I raced according to plan.

Paul experienced a sense of completion at the end of his life, not simply because he lived a long time, but because he was through with what he had set out to do. He ran according to plan.

Nobody plans to fail. But, as the saying goes, "If you fail to plan, you plan to fail." People without a plan get to the end empty, full of regret, wishing they had done more. They didn't plan so they didn't finish.

The Bible uses words like *redeem*, *restore*, *renew*, *revive*, and *replenish* to describe what God wants to do in our lives. These things don't happen in a sprint. God created the world in 6 days, but according to the Biblical record of redemptive history, He has been working for thousands of years to rescue it. Redemption and renewal do not come easy. You and I have a long way to go. There are a lot of events and experiences that will be part of the process. Much like a triathlon, in order to accomplish our purpose, we may be required to change our mode of transportation at different points along the way. However your walk fleshes out, the key is not going fast. Success is in going far - for the rest of your life - all the way to the finish.

You may agree wholeheartedly with everything written in this book. You may affirm it, knowing that doing life at walking pace, step by step, would be a much better way to live than the way you are living now. You may even appreciate the Scripture references and the truths shared about Christ and the gospel. But let's be honest for a moment - what's your plan?

Remember something stated earlier, "L*ip service is not life change.*"

I often deal with people who have great intentions but constant sorrows because nothing ever changes. They believe strongly, but their schedule is never adjusted. They pray fervently, but sacrifice nothing. I see people all the time who hear truth and their faces light up with excitement. It is a true *ah-ha* kind of a moment for them. There is information, but there is no plan. Despite the information, these people don't get very far, and they are a long way from being finished with satisfaction.

If you are going to walk with God, I hope you have gleaned from the book, you can't simply add something else to your already-going-way-too-fast life. Yet, to walk with God, we need to be in the Scriptures. We need time to think before we act. We need to meditate on Scripture, receive less notifications on our smartphone, and take more notice of what is going on around us. We need to give time to gospel-centered community. We need to take inventory of our lives, where we are, what we have, and why we are where we are. We'll never do the things the Bible teaches us about walking with God if it merely becomes something else we have to do.

To recall another statement I made in the opening chapter, the Bible teaches that the decision to walk with God is life altering. The word *walk* in the Bible did not describe something the people of the times did; the word *walk* was used to describe everything they did. Walking was synonymous with life.

Understanding this principle leads us to two critical applications about our plan to walk: 1) the plan of salvation and 2) the plan for the next step.

Without knowing Christ as Savior, the walk becomes merely a set of moral suggestions that are doomed to fail. The lifestyle of Scripture reading, meditation, purity, community, etc., done incredibly well by the most sincere people merits nothing with God. To recall yet another statement in the opening chapter, our walk was ruined by sin.

God created a world that was perfectly good and well suited for life (Gen. 1). Man was created in the image of God to subdue the earth, to multiply, and to fill it for His glory (Gen. 2). In short, we were to grow the garden. We were to bring the planet to full fruit and spread the goodness of God's grace and rule over creation. As the images of God, man was not only to reflect who Creator was, but as image, man was God's deputy. Wherever man was, he was to do what God would do in that place as if He were there Himself.

In Genesis 3 that plan was tragically interrupted. Man sinned against God. His desire was to be like God, knowing good and evil. Instead of becoming "like God" in a way that enhanced his life, man reaped death and was destined to return to the dust from which he came (Gen. 3:19). Yet, all was not lost.

A theme of hope entered the story as God pronounced a curse upon the serpent. The woman, who with the man was destined to death, would retain the blessing of birth. Though birth and childrearing would be more painful and difficult, there would be a son born from the woman who would suffer, but would somehow crush the curse (Gen. 3:15).

The bulk of the Bible is the story of the coming of this saving son. Many sons were born in the Old Testament. Patriarchs, prophets, and powerful kings all emerge on the scene. Many of them fostered hope, but all of them were fatally flawed. None were able to deliver on God's promise, and the world grew more divided and dangerous. By the end of the Old Testament, even the kingdom of God's people, Israel, looked destined for extinction. For a time, about 400 years, the story grows silent. What will become of the saving son?

The silence is broken as the angels convey a message to a virgin girl, her betrothed husband, and eventually to shepherds abiding in the field (Luke 2). The saving son is born. His name is Jesus, and He demonstrates the power to reverse the curse. He heals the sick and even raises the dead. All the curse has done to man, the saving son is able to rescue and redeem.

As hopeful as the presence of the saving son becomes, opposition grows and in a surprising twist the saving son is crucified on a Roman cross (Luke 22-23). It appears that any hope of deliverance for mankind dies with the one we thought was to be the saving son.

Yet, what man meant for evil, God meant for good. In His death on the cross, Jesus became the ultimate sacrifice for our sins. He bore in His death what we deserve in our sinful life. He paid the price for our sins and satisfied God's wrath against us. He took our place. Three days later Jesus is raised from the dead, forever securing His role as the saving son.

Jesus stayed on earth forty days after His resurrection, showing Himself alive to many (1 Corinthians 15). He then ascended to Heaven (Acts 1). Ten days later He fulfilled His promise to pour out His Holy Spirit on His people. This happened on a scheduled feast day known as Pentecost to the Jewish people (Acts 2).

The resurrection of Christ and the pouring out of His Spirit is the dawning of a new age. In fact, it is the final stage of God's grand plan. In this final act, God is gathering for Himself a people from every nation who believe upon His Son, the saving son, and who are filled with His Spirit. In the end, these people will be rescued from judgment and will enter a new Heaven and a new earth. The curse will finally be reversed, and the story returns to its original intent. The images of God, mankind, will return to the wonderful work of demonstrating the wonderful rule of God over His creation (Revelation 20 and 21). What was lost in the beginning is redeemed in the end.

Are you one of those people?

The Bible teaches that the gift of eternal life in Jesus Christ is received through repentance and faith (Romans 3:23, 5:8, 6:23, 10:9-10, 13, Ephesians 2:1-10). John 3 is a simple explanation to a brilliant man of what it means to be born again. There, Jesus tells the accomplished intellect, Nicodemus, that to enter the Kingdom of Heaven, you must be born again (John 3:3).

Salvation is not achieved, it is received. Again, you can execute every principle of this book perfectly, but, unless you repent of sin and believe upon Jesus Christ as Savior, you will not enter the Kingdom with Him.

Because we have sinned, we have forfeited our rights to enter the Kingdom of Heaven. Because of Adam's sin, we are born into sin. Everything about us, from our motives to our actions, is stained with sin. Nothing about us is pure. The Bible says that even the best we do is polluted (Isaiah 64:6).

Thinking we can do enough to merit salvation is like holding a full cup of water *below* an empty bucket and attempting to fill it up. You may try repeatedly, but y*ou can't possibly fill it up because you can't possibly pour it up*. Pouring water up goes against the laws of nature. A sinner thinking he can become deserving of salvation is against nature. It just doesn't work.

To be saved, you must repent of sin, believe upon Jesus as Savior and receive His gift of eternal life. Salvation is not about what you can do for Him. Salvation is about what He has done for you.

The greatest plan of all is God's plan of salvation. If you do not first respond to that plan, the rest of your plans will be brought to nothing. Without Christ, your desire to go further will end in eternal failure. If you have not received Christ as Savior, I encourage you to pray and ask for His mercy and forgiveness right now. If you need further clarification, read the Book of John in the Bible. Find a friend or someone you know who follows Jesus with their lives and ask them what it means to be saved.

As a Christ follower, the rest of your life is to be characterized by walking with God. For the disciple, the things we have talked about in this book are not things we do to merely learn about God. They are things that will bring peace to your life, but we do not do them merely for peace. Doing these things will help you go further by deepening your relationship with your wife, investing more of yourself in your children, thinking and praying about decisions in life and business instead of rushing through it. But improvement is not the goal. Walking with God is about application. We do what we do because we want life to become, as Paul said in 1 Thessalonians 4:1, "more and more" pleasing to God.

When I learned to focus less on destination and more on details, less on the future and more on today, it revolutionized my walk. I no longer whine to God about where I want to be; I seek wisdom from God for where I am. I have only one question about every plan in my life, no matter how big or how small: What's next? That simple question in prayer, "What's next?" has revolutionized my life.

I can't be thinking about all that tomorrow holds when my daughters need me to speak into their lives over dinner tonight. I need to pace myself so that I am present.

I don't ask God what He wants me to do with my life. I ask God what He wants me to do with the day.

I can't answer every text message or respond to every notification that is on my smartphone. Most of it is a distraction. God has placed things all around me He wants me to see throughout the day. He wants me to interpret life, not with a phone in my face, but by the meditations of Scripture that are still reverberating in my heart.

The principles in this book are timeless. I encourage you make a plan for assimilating them into your life. Read the book again. Read it along with someone close to you. Make notes. Investigate the contexts of the Scripture references. Take your time. Go further.

You have a good God who wants you to end up in a good place. Walk with Him.

Endnotes

1 Kevin DeYoung, (2013-09-23). *Crazy Busy: A (Mercifully) Short Book about a (Really) Big Problem* (Kindle Location 837). Crossway. Kindle Edition.

2 Ibid. (Kindle Locations 898-903).

3 Philip Graham Ryken, *Jeremiah and Lamentations, From Sorrow to Hope* (Wheaton, IL: Crossway, 2001), 107.

4 Bruce K. Waltke, *The Book of Proverbs, Chapters 1–15, The New International Commentary on the Old Testament* (Grand Rapids, MI: Wm. B. Eerdmans Publishing Co., 2004), 243.

5 Francis Brown, Samuel Rolles Driver, and Charles Augustus Briggs, *Enhanced Brown-Driver-Briggs Hebrew and English Lexicon* (Oak Harbor, WA: Logos Research Systems, 2000), 393.

6 Gemma Aldridge and Kerry Harden, *The Mirror*, "Selfie addict took two hundred a day, and tried to kill himself when he couldn't take the perfect photo" http://www.mirror.co.uk/news/real-life-stories/selfie-addict-took-two-hundred-3273819 Accessed 4/12/2014

7 See "Selfies, Self-deception, and Self Worship" *The Gospel Coalition* http://thegospelcoalition.org/blogs/tgcworship/2014/02/21/selfies-self-deception-and-self-worship/ accessed 4/11/2014.

8 Sarah Brooks, *Life as of Late* "Parents: A Word about Instagram" http://lifeasoflate.com/2013/04/parents-a-word-about-instagram.html accessed 4/11/2014.

9 See "Selfies, Self-deception, and Self Worship" *The Gospel Coalition* http://thegospelcoalition.org/blogs/tgcworship/2014/02/21/selfies-self-deception-and-self-worship/ accessed 4/11/2014.

10 John Piper, *Desiring God, Meditations of a Christian Hedonist*, (Colorado Springs, CO: Multnomah Books, 2011), 33.

[11] Lyle W. Dorsett ed., *The Essential C.S. Lewis*, (New York, NY: Scribner, 1996), 362.

[12] Francis Brown, 164.

[13] The Mountain Crossings Store, http://www.mountaincrossings.com/aboutus.asp (accessed 5/2/2014)

[14] Tom Mangan, Two Heel Drive, a Hiking Blog, "Blood Mountain Loop and Neel's Gap on the Appalachain Trail." http://www.tommangan.net/twoheeldrive/index.php/2011/06/24/blood-mountain-loop-and-neels-gap-on-the-appalachian-trail/ accessed 5/2/2014

[15] For a thorough explanation of many of the concepts of this chapter, please see *The Theology of Work Project* http://www.theologyofwork.org/key-topics/provision-wealth/. (Accessed 5/2/2014).

[16] http://www.theologyofwork.org/key-topics/provision-wealth/

[17] Theology of Work Project - *Faith in God's Provision,* http://www.theologyofwork.org/old-testament/jeremiah-lamentations/work-related-themes-in-the-book-of-jeremiah/faith-in-gods-provision-jeremiah-8-16//, accessed 5/2/14.

[18] Daniel Aiken, Bruce Riley Ashford, and Kenneth Keathley. "The Doctrine of Salvation." *A Theology for the Church.* (Nashville: B&H Publishing, 2007), 754.

[19] It was common for men in Greek culture to have not only a wife who would bear their children, but a mistress who he would present in public.

[20] *Morality in Media*, Porn Harms Research, http://pornharmsresearch.com, accessed 5/12/14.

34347242R00102

Made in the USA
Charleston, SC
07 October 2014